Costume Society of America series

Phyllis A. Specht,
Series Editor

ALSO IN THE COSTUME SOCIETY OF AMERICA SERIES

YOUNG ORIGINALS

Rebecca Jumper Matheson

Emily Wilkens and the Teen Sophisticate

YOUNG ORIGINALS

Texas Tech University Press

This book is typeset in Minion Pro. The paper used in this book meets the minimum requirements of ANSI/NISO Z39.48-1992 (R1997). ∞

Designed by Kasey McBeath

Library of Congress Cataloging-in-Publication Data
Matheson, Rebecca Jumper, 1975-
    Young Originals : Emily Wilkens and the teen sophisticate / Rebecca Jumper Matheson.
        pages cm. — (Costume society of America series)
    Includes bibliographical references and index.
    ISBN 978-0-89672-924-7 (paperback) — ISBN 978-0-89672-925-4 (e-book) 1. Wilkens, Emily. 2. Women fashion designers—United States—Biography. 3. Fashion designers—United States—Biography. 4. Fashion illustrators—United States—Biography. 5. Teenage girls—Clothing—United States—History—20th century. 6. Fashion merchandising—United States—History—20th century. 7. Fashion—United States—History—20th century. 8. Beauty, Personal—Social aspects—United States—History—20th century. I. Title.
        TT505.W54M38 2015
        746.9'2092—dc23
        [B]
                                                    2014047391

15 16 17 18 19 20 21 22 23 / 9 8 7 6 5 4 3 2 1

Texas Tech University Press
Box 41037 | Lubbock, Texas 79409-1037 USA
800.832.4042 | ttup@ttu.edu | www.ttupress.org

"*Fashion and Costume Sketch Collection. Emily Wilkens sketch 041-06, Spring 1946.*" 1946. Brooklyn Museum Libraries. Fashion and Costume Sketch Collection. Special Collections.

CONTENTS

ILLUSTRATIONS

I n a temperature- and humidity-controlled room in the basement of one of the world's greatest art museums, I huddled in my lab coat and encountered my first Emily Wilkens dress. And another and another. . . . There was a blue dress—tiny and delicate but with simple lines and a nosegay of faded flowers at the waistband. Was that an evening dress made of reddish-pink-and-white cotton stripes, ruffled at the hem and gathered into a big bow and a bustle at the back? A bright yellow day dress, undimmed by the passing years, showed the sharp contrast of black ribbon trim. The garments were beautiful, with an accessible aesthetic. My curiosity was piqued. I went home and added a yellow folder titled "Emily Wilkens" to my fashion-designer files.

It would be several years before I would begin more focused research on the work of Wilkens, and it has been a fascinating journey. There are many people I would like to thank, beginning with Wilkens's family. To Hugh Wilkens Levey and Jane Wilkens Michael I owe tremendous thanks for granting me permission to publish Emily Wilkens's sketches, ephemera, and other materials still owned by the family. This book would not have been possible without their support, and I am extremely grateful. Jane and her husband, Robert Michael, have gone above and beyond in making the Emily Wilkens materials available for my research, including retrieving items from storage and allowing me to borrow materials for several years during my research. These family members have all generously shared their time and memories of Emily Wilkens with me. Jane has been an invaluable resource and a wonderful encourager.

ACKNOWLEDGMENTS

I would also like to acknowledge Emily Wilkens's descendants in later generations: her grandchildren, Evan Levey, Mariel Levey, Alex Michael, Elise Michael, and Philip Michael; and great-grandchildren, Aliza Rose Michael and Zoey Eleanor Michael.

Emily Wilkens once told her daughter Jane about working during one of her pregnancies; she commentated a fashion show from behind a large podium to disguise her expanding waistline. I smiled to myself when I heard this story, remembering how in June 2011 I presented a paper about Wilkens at the National Symposium of the Costume Society of America, a huge wooden podium obscuring the "baby bump" that was my daughter Priscilla. It was after I presented this paper that Texas Tech University Press Assistant Director Judith Keeling (now retired) suggested that I expand my research into a book about Wilkens. I am very grateful to Judith for her vision of this book and her contribution to the field of fashion studies during her years at Texas Tech University Press. I also would like to thank Judith for continuing to work as my editor once she returned part-time to the Press post-retirement.

Many thanks to Phyllis Specht, the Costume Society of America Series Editor. A big thank you also to Courtney Burkholder, the new director of Texas Tech University Press, and Joanna Conrad, the new assistant director and editor-in-chief. Thank you to Amanda Werts and Rachel Murdy, and to Sandra Spicher for her careful copyediting.

Portions of this book first appeared in the *2010 Proceedings of the Dublin Seminar for New England Folklife: Dressing New England: Clothing, Fashion, and Identity*, in a paper titled "Emily Wilkens: New England Designer for All-American Teens." Thank you very much to Peter Benes and Dublin Seminar for New England Folklife for kind permission to publish this material.

I would like to thank the following individuals at various institutions who assisted with research appointments and image permissions: Brooklyn Museum Library—Deirdre Lawrence and Dyani Scheuerman; Condé Nast Archive—Marianne Brown and Leigh Montville; the Costume Institute, The Metropolitan Museum of Art—Elizabeth Bryan; Eileen Darby Images, Inc.—Alex Teslik; Fairchild Archive—Molly Monosky; Fashion Institute of Technology, Gladys Marcus Library, Special Collections—Karen Cannell, Juliet Jacobson; Museum of the City of New York—Nilda Rivera; Museum of Modern Art—Jennifer Tobias; The New York Public Library—Thomas Lisanti; Pratt Institute—Paul Schlotthauer, Gina Shelton. Thank you to Leslie Greaves for permission to publish Murray Korman's photograph of Wilkens.

The staff of the Valentine Richmond History Center were all incredibly gracious and helpful when I visited for my research appointment. I was delighted to be present for the photo shoot of their Emily Wilkens Young Originals dress. I would like to thank Meghan Glass-Hughes, Jackie Finney Mullins, and Autumn Reinhardt-Simpson for all their help and for making that such a special day.

The garments that formed my introduction to Wilkens's work are now in the collection of Parsons, the New School of Design. Unfortunately, these garments have not been available for research during the period when I have been working on this book. I would like to thank the Parsons collection's curator, Beth Charleston, for keeping me up-to-date on the status of these garments.

The project of photographing private-collection garments for this book was a collaborative undertaking, and I am very grateful for the talented contributions of several people. At the School of Graduate Studies of my alma mater, the Fashion Institute of Technology, I owe a huge thank you to Denyse Montegut, Chair of the Fashion and Textile Studies master's program, who was wonderfully generous in allowing me to use space and mannequins for object photography. Many thanks also to Ewa Garbos, Industry/Department Project Coordinator for the department, for her help. For the day of photography, I would like to thank Kathryn Squitieri and Lolly Koon, both a pleasure to work with. Kathryn dressed the garments beautifully. Lolly's gorgeous photographs really bring the objects to life; they showcase her sensitivity to the textiles and her skill in bringing out the best in each garment.

For the writer who is also the mother of young children, a truly crucial element is childcare. I would like to thank our babysitters during the hours when I was researching and writing, who have all been exemplary role models for our daughters: Leah Cravenho, Stephanie Gamboa, Rebecca Marshall, Laurel Recsetar, and Elisabeth Turner. Rebecca Marshall assisted me over the two summers when I was working most intensely in the preparation of this manuscript, so I owe her particular thanks.

I would also like to thank my parents, Jack and Dana Jumper, who have always encouraged me in my work. Special thanks to my sister Rachel Leah Jumper for advice and resources concerning adolescent development. To my wonderful husband, Dan Matheson, and our precious girls Elizabeth Grace and Priscilla Leah—thank you and much love.

Above all, I give thanks and all glory to God.

"Not to us, O Lord, not to us but to your name be the glory, because of your love and faithfulness" Psalm 115:1 (NIV).

"And whatever you do, whether in word or deed, do it all in the name of the Lord Jesus, giving thanks to God the Father through him" Colossians 3:17 (NIV).

In the darkened ballroom of New York City's Waldorf-Astoria hotel, a stage hung with pale blue curtains glowed with a soft blue light like something out of *Swan Lake*. One thousand audience members waited in hushed anticipation. It was a fashionable crowd, and not just terms of personal chic, their tailored daytime suits contrasting with a bit of whimsical millinery on their heads. Many of the spectators there to watch the American Fashion Critics Awards presentation on that February midday in 1945 were involved in the business of American fashion. Their faces were serious. The wartime American ready-to-wear industry depended on a careful balance of consumerism and caution, regulation and promotion.

A single spotlight swung around to illuminate the next models in the parade, teenage girls showing the work of a young illustrator-turned-fashion-designer named Emily Wilkens. The models of fellow honorees Tina Leser and Gilbert Adrian would walk with a cool elegance that mirrored the general perception of the woman of fashion: she was mature, sophisticated, a thirty-something with time to cultivate her appearance. Wilkens's models bounded onto the stage with a burst of adolescent energy and proceeded to skip along the winding runway, which curved beyond the stage and into the audience seating area.

The Wilkens models carried teenage culture props, such as a gigantic ice cream soda and an oversize record. They showed mix-and-match separates ensembles, day dresses, and even a diaphanous "dream dress" with layers of wedding-cake ruffles for evening. Throughout her presentation, Wilkens demonstrated one of her great strengths: creating historicizing yet modern clothes. She took elements of nineteenth-century fashion, such as eyelet trim, and married them to contemporary sportswear forms like the playsuit. Her "young black" dresses pushed the boundaries of what was respectable and appropriate teenage garb.

The well-known publicist Eleanor Lambert wrote that "[t]o win a Coty Award, a fashion designer must in the previous year have been an outstanding contributor to contemporary American style, or a new talent whose ideas point the way to significant future change in American dress."[1] Wilkens certainly fit within the scope of both, as an emerging talent whose work anticipated the increasing importance of the teenager on the American fashion scene and fashion's growing new emphasis on youth. Contrary to popular wisdom, Wilkens's designs declared that a very young woman—even a teenager—*could* be fashionable. In doing so, Wilkens laid the foundation for the seismic shift that would occur later in the twentieth century, when youth became the fashionable ideal.

In the space of a very few years in the 1940s, Wilkens skyrocketed from obscurity to national recognition. She was an entrepreneur and partner in her own company, a fashion designer with her name on the label of each Emily Wilkens Young Original. Yet today even many fashion insiders would not recognize her name. In so many areas, Wilkens was ahead of her time. We think of spas, yoga, and organic food as twenty-first-century trends, yet Wilkens was already at the vanguard of these movements half a century ago.

Wilkens was one of the first American fashion designers to recognize the growing importance of the teenage girl in American culture and to design specifically for this emerging category of consumers. Wilkens strived toward a youthful ideal throughout her long and varied career in the world of fashion and beauty.

This book will trace the history of Wilkens's life and career. Chapter one recounts Wilkens's childhood and early years. Who doesn't have at least one memory of an awkward stage on the road to adulthood? Wilkens used her own "ugly duckling" memory of badly fitting dresses as inspiration for improving the lives of teenage girls across the nation, through good design.

Chapter two will recount the rise of the teenager, from turn-of-the-twentieth-century ideas about the adolescent developmental stage to the 1940s concept of the teenager. This chapter uses Sally Benson's *Junior Miss*—print, stage, and screen versions—as a vehicle for analyzing what American teen girls were wearing just prior to the United States' entry into World War II, in order to understand the context in which Wilkens's teen-size designs evolved.

Chapter three tells the story of how Wilkens, as entrepreneur, sought a mass-market solution to the young teenager's fashion difficulties—a solution firmly grounded in the framework of American ready-to-wear. One of Wilkens's significant contributions to American fashion revolves around the history of her business. In this chapter I will explore the unique business relationship she enjoyed with garment manufacturers Roy and Ben Chalk, a partnership that allowed her to exert agency by retaining both fiscal and artistic control over her own label, Emily Wilkens Young Originals. I will discuss the significance of her name on the garment label, as well as other key elements of the Emily Wilkens Young Originals business, such as the fabric-supply deal she struck with Everfast and the many design patents she filed to protect her dress designs.

If all fashion begins with an ideal body, then it is important to understand a designer's ideal in order to fully grasp her work. Wilkens had a clear and consistent ideal of beauty throughout her career, and fortunately for us, she spent much of the second half of her career writing about it. The Wilkens look can be summarized as youthful, clean, tidy, and healthy. Chapter four examines consistent themes in the advice literature Wilkens wrote concerning her ideal of beauty, including personal evaluation, diet, exercise, grooming, general wellness, and wardrobe.

Chapter five details how Wilkens translated her ideal of beauty into garments even before she recorded her thoughts in writing. I will discuss the specific design features Wilkens created for teenagers of the 1940s, including shoulder wings, expandable waistlines, and hems to let out—all elements which were supposed to camouflage teen "figure flaws" and to work practically with growing and developing bodies. This chapter will also consider how Wilkens met the creative challenges posed by wartime restrictions from government agencies such as the War Production Board and Office of Price Administration. Finally, I will discuss "young black" and Wilkens's negotiation of fashion etiquette regarding the fabric color choices of teenagers and the issues of too-early sophistication.

It was in this area of negotiating between societal expectations and teenage desires that Wilkens truly excelled. As chapter six shows, Wilkens's blend of modern and historicizing elements in her fashions for teenagers both pleased teens and reassured not just the parents of teenage daughters but the American public in general. In this chapter, the Broadway play *Dear Ruth* will be used to show how the years of the Second World War allowed teenage girls in the United States to flourish, exerting more agency than ever before. Americans were ambivalent about this: on one hand proud of these young women as emblematic of the ideals being fought for in the war, while longing to protect teenagers' innocence and keep them from growing up too fast. Wilkens's work was grounded both in the principles of modernism common to American sportswear, such as functionality, and also in American history through museum research—one of the sources to which American designers turned for inspiration once cut off from the Paris couture. It is this combination of female agency and American tradition that both the fashion industry and the American public found so uniquely reassuring in 1944 and 1945, leading to Wilkens's many awards and accolades.

A crucial aspect of fashion success in every era is publicity. Chapter seven links marketing efforts for Emily Wilkens Young Originals to an overview of the developments in fashion marketing to teenagers in general in the 1940s. For example, Wilkens worked with publicist Eleanor Lambert, who was instrumental in making many American designers household names. Wilkens's business also coincided with the growing awareness of teenage girls as independently acting consumers, which led to the emergence of fashion magazines specifically aimed at high school–age teenagers, such as *Seventeen*, and stand-alone issues of *Junior Bazaar*. The relatively new field of public relations was also making inroads at department stores, where fashion shows, teen departments, and teen clubs were used to draw young consumers and build store loyalty in the years before they shopped for trousseaus. Furthermore, stores like Bonwit Teller and G. Fox & Co. featured named Emily Wilkens sections, and Wilkens built excitement for her brand through in-store appearances.

But the story of Wilkens's 1940s success also fits within the broader picture of American history, fashion history, and women's studies. Chapter eight follows Wilkens as World War II ended. She married and closed the Emily Wilkens Young Originals business and then struggled to find the right balance between the demands of family and her creative impulses. Wilkens did find time to design clothing in the 1950s, working for stores or manufacturers rather than running her own business. Her family still owns one of her books of sketches for Bonwit Teller, and this will serve as a foundation for examining her postwar designs.

Chapter nine moves into the final stage of Wilkens's career, in the 1960s and beyond, as she reinvented herself as a college teacher, lecturer, columnist, beauty guru, and spa expert. One of Wilkens's great talents was to identify up-and-coming trends and to see how she could fruitfully express her own interests within those contexts. A creative person overflowing with ideas and energy, Wilkens remained true to her own ideal of beauty while adapting her focus for each decade.

YOUNG ORIGINALS

Figure 1. Emily Wilkens as a baby, c. 1917. Photographer unknown.
Courtesy of Hugh Wilkens Levey and Jane Wilkens Michael.

FAMILY HISTORY AND EDUCATION

Emily Ann Wilkens was born on May 6, 1917 (Fig. 1). Wilkens did not care for her middle name, and it rarely appears in her press coverage.[1] She was the first child of Lithuanian and Russian Jewish immigrants Morris Wilkens and Rose Drey Wilkens[2] (Figs. 2, 3). Approximately one-third of Europe's Jewish population immigrated to the United States in the nineteenth century and early twentieth century; Wilkens's family had been part of this movement.[3] Morris and Rose Wilkens made their home and raised their family in West Hartford, Connecticut.[4]

Emily Wilkens's daughter, Jane Michael, recalls the blonde, blue-eyed Rose being a proponent of healthy foods, making her own carrot juice and borsht.[5] Rose also seems to have had some interest in clothing—she knitted suits and coats for her young daughter Emily.[6]

According to journalist Beryl Williams, writing in 1945, Morris Wilkens worked in real estate.[7] The renowned publicist Eleanor Lambert, in a press release six years later, would state that Wilkens was "the daughter of a successful pharmacist."[8] It seems that both are correct, with Emily's father a trained pharmacist with a flair for fruitful dabbling in real estate.[9]

Wilkens would later describe her father as "a scientist" who was interested in anti-aging treatments de-

Figure 2. (left) Rose Drey Wilkens in her wedding dress, c. 1915. Photographer unknown. Courtesy of Hugh Wilkens Levey and Jane Wilkens Michael.
Figure 3. (right) Morris Wilkens, 1947. Photographer unknown.
Courtesy of Hugh Wilkens Levey and Jane Wilkens Michael.

veloped in Switzerland: "He spoke with great admiration about Dr. Paul Niehans' cellular therapy. My father believed ways could be found to prolong our lives and keep us younger longer, and so he was interested in Dr. Niehans' finding."[10] Morris Wilkens's interest in anti-aging treatments and the pursuit of youthfulness must have made an impression on his young daughter; she would one day make beauty and spa treatments, including taking cellular-therapy injections, the focus of her career.

Emily Wilkens grew up in a time when the cosmetics industry was expanding, and she was certainly affected by these marketing messages. The idea that women could take control of their beauty destiny with effort and the application of the right cosmetics was pervasive during Wilkens's childhood in the 1920s. Home economist Christine Frederick, in her 1929 book *Selling Mrs. Consumer,* noted that one of the areas of American consumer spending that was fast increasing was "toilet goods." Frederick also observed that even the rural young woman "whose face was formerly innocent of aught but freckles, now possesses our standard laboratory of toilet articles and not one, but *several* types of face creams and powders!"[11]

Beauty-product marketing reached across divisions of class and population density.

During Wilkens's teen years in the early 1930s, the beauty industry began to advertise more directly to teenagers.[12] Wilkens would later acknowledge the effects of this advertising: "My generation of Americans was conditioned to be perpetually anxious about offending with their 'b.o.' We blocked or masked personal smells with a bevy of deodorants and anti-perspirants, plus perfumes, colognes, and toilet waters."[13] When the adult Wilkens counseled teenagers (and later, adults) on the keys to attractiveness, she was speaking from an ideal of beauty that she had internalized and made part of her day-to-day life. This made her especially persuasive.

Wilkens was to be the oldest child among four siblings.[14] She had a brother, Bernard ("Bern") born in 1923, followed by sisters Barbara (1929) and Janet (1933).[15] The Wilkens children may have had a Swiss governess, who would take them for walks beside pine trees on the theory that air from the pine trees was healing.[16]

It is significant that both of Emily Wilkens's younger sisters were born more than ten years after her: Barbara and Janet were young teenagers in the early 1940s—they were part of the same demographic that would be Emily Wilkens Young Originals customers. Both of Wilkens's sisters would figure in her first book, *Here's Looking at . . . You!*, but particularly Barbara is used as a sort of vehicle to trace the application of Emily Wilkens's formula for beauty and to show its success.[17]

As a child, the vividly red-haired Emily was small for her age, wearing a size six dress at age eight.[18] She wore a combination of purchased ready-to-wear clothes and garments that her mother made for her, as well as the occasional gift of Parisian dresses from a relative in Europe.[19]

Emily Wilkens would later state that the awkward stage she went through at age thirteen, when she had a "pudgy teenage waistline under a bunchy 'kid's dress,'" was the personal experience that led her to address what she viewed as typical teenage figure flaws in her designs.[20] It is also evidence of the pressure that women were experiencing, even at a young age, to conform to an ideal of beauty—whether this arose from social sources or from the early-twentieth-century marketing campaigns that were already attempting to convince young consumers that their products were needed to achieve beauty.

Wilkens would indeed grow out of her awkward stage to become a

Figure 4. Emily Wilkens, 1943. Photograph by Murray Korman. Courtesy of Leslie Greaves.

beautiful woman (Fig. 4). Her publicist, Lambert, would describe Wilkens as an adult as having a "delicate 'junior size' figure, big hazel eyes [and] red-gold hair."[21] The cosmetics mogul Estée Lauder counted Wilkens among her friends, and Lauder would later recall that Wilkens "was acknowledged to be one of the great beauties of her time. . . ."[22]

Like growing numbers of young women in the early twentieth century, Emily Wilkens attended high school, where students were grouped by age rather than by level of progress (as had been in the case in nineteenth-century "one-room-schoolhouse" models of education). She graduated from Hartford's Weaver High School[23] (Fig. 5). Despite her family's wishes for her to attend Smith College, Wilkens decided to go to art school.[24] Illness forced her to stay in her hometown and take art classes at Hartford Art School for a year.[25] She then enrolled in the three-year program in fashion illustration—a division of the advertising design department—at Pratt Institute in Brooklyn, New York. However, when she arrived at Pratt she was allowed to proceed directly into the second-year courses.[26]

One anecdote that Wilkens recounted both to Beryl Williams in 1945

Figure 5. Emily Wilkens was one of a growing number of twentieth-century American teenagers who graduated from high school. Postcard. H. P. Kopplemann, Pub. Agent. "Weaver High School, Hartford, Conn." Postmark 31 July 1947. Author's collection.

and later to her family involved criticism of her work. Wilkens would re-call a teacher—either from art class at Weaver High or one of her college illustration professors—who (intentionally or unintentionally) gave her particular motivation. In criticizing one of Wilkens's sketches, the instruc-tor declared that the hand she had drawn looked like a dog's paw. Wilkens determined to prove the teacher wrong by showing that she could draw well enough to find work in the field.[27] However, it is interesting to note that in her sketches, hands are often minimized—by hiding in pockets [Plates 1, 2], by holding a distracting bouquet of flowers [Plate 3], or by other devices.

One commentator later reported, "While she [Emily Wilkens] was still in school she had a careful series of drawings illustrating the history of costume, and she has often and gratefully returned to them for inspiration since."[28] Historicism was to become one of the signature elements of the Wilkens style.

Wilkens's *Prattonia* yearbook picture shows a youthful Wilkens with her hair styled in a manner that anticipates the hairdos of the 1940s—

WILKENS, EMILY. 2199 Main St., Hartford, Conn. Riding Club '37; Modern Dance '37, '38; Fencing '37; Volleyball '37. "Four and Five Times."

Figure 6. Emily Wilkens's college yearbook picture, from the 1938 *Prattonia*. Wilkens is in the second row, third from left. Reproduced by permission of Pratt Institute Archives.

parted in the center, with rolls on either side of the head (Fig. 6). Wilkens was already showing her aptitude for beauty, but her interests were well-rounded enough to include several extracurricular sports such as riding, fencing, and volleyball. She participated in modern dance both of her years at Pratt. Wilkens's yearbook entry includes her hometown address—2199 Main St. (just north of downtown Hartford, and about three miles from Weaver High School)—as well as the title of a song, "Four and Five Times."[29]

Records in the Office of the Registrar at Pratt Institute show that Wilkens received a certificate in fashion illustration under the School of Fine and Applied Arts on June 9, 1938.[30] Twenty-one-year-old Wilkens then began her job search. The young graduate did prove her critical instructor wrong, securing her first job as a fashion artist, sketching dresses for department-store newspaper ads.[31]

EARLY CAREER AND HOLLYWOOD

While today we tend to lump all fashion drawings together under the name "illustration," in the mid-twentieth-century there were divisions within this type of work. The broader term "fashion art" (sometimes used interchangeably with "illustration") included both drawings of specific ensembles provided by a client and the work of "illustration" (used in the more specific sense) in which the fashion artist used imagination in drawing garments, as in institutional advertising promoting the image of a magazine, store, or company.[32]

Wilkens's first job as a fashion artist included one sketch per week for King Features Syndicate, drawing garments for retail advertisers such as Jane Engel, Macy's, and Lord & Taylor. She also did "illustrations of young people's clothes for such magazines as *The New Yorker* and *Mademoiselle*."[33] However, in 1940, Wilkens lost her fashion art job for taking too many artistic liberties in her interpretations of the designs—in essence, she was drawing her own designs rather than the garments actually in front of her.[34] This might have simply pointed her back to the "illustration" work used for institutional advertising, but instead she used it as a springboard to a different area of the fashion industry.

Wilkens then went to California, where she was (by mistake) introduced to people in the motion picture industry as a New York designer and found work designing movie costumes for child star Ann Todd.[35] Fashion journalist Beryl Williams described Wilkens's rapport with the young star:

> The little actress was especially pleased because Emily talked to her seriously, to find out just what sort of things she wanted to wear, and what sort of clothes would best express Ann's personality. And then she sketched a whole series of ensembles—not just dresses, but coats to go with them, and hats and bags and gloves that matched—and put all the sketches into a beautiful scrapbook with Ann's name on the cover. Ann could use it, Emily explained, as a sort of clothes diary."[36]

In these custom costume designs, Wilkens followed the example of early-twentieth-century couturiere Lucile, Lady Duff Gordon, whose early work included "personal dresses" intended to reflect the individual personality of the client.[37] The movie for which Ann Todd's costumes were planned was never released, but this project led to Wilkens doing noncostume design work for other Hollywood children, including Melinda Markey (daughter of Joan Bennett), Sandra Burns (adopted daughter of Gracie Allen and George Burns), and Joan Benny (daughter of Mary Livingston and Jack Benny).[38] Wilkens's foray into custom childrenswear was done in the name of children's agency—Wilkens wrote that she had noticed that while adult women of Hollywood dressed to suit their individual personalities, their daughters were dressed in generic clothes just like little girls all over the country. Wilkens planned to create clothes that allowed girls to express themselves.[39] She described making notebooks for each child:

> I started each with a wardrobe plan and gave each child a small pink and white notebook tied with a green velvet ribbon, containing pictures of their dresses. With each child's dress I made a matching dress for her doll so that she could have the fun of superintending a doll wardrobe just like her own. I remember that Melinda Markey had a charming little plaid dress and gloves, a matching dress for her doll, and even a matching coat for her dog.[40]

Long before American Girl advertised Dress Like Your Doll clothes, Wilkens created matching clothes for girls and dolls in which the agency of the child was paramount: the doll matched the girl, not the other way around.[41] Writing in 1947, Bernice Chambers of the Fashion Group and assistant professor at New York University, noted that Wilkens's sketches in the wardrobe notebooks were not just of the dresses, but "of each little customer in the dress designed for her."[42]

Due to her early training in illustration, sketching would remain key to Wilkens's design process.[43] In this, Wilkens was similar to fellow American designer Muriel King, who also began as a fashion artist.[44] A 1945 House Beautiful article from Sara Little's "Girl with a Future" series shows Wilkens working in her small studio apartment in New York. In the photos, Wilkens sketches new dress designs surrounded by two dressmaker's dummies (one miniature scale, the other life-size wearing a highly shoulder-padded blouse or bodice), sketches pinned to the wall, a hat, a hair-band, and a handbag. In the foreground are two sketches with swatches of fabric attached.[45]

Figure 7. Emily Wilkens was already being advertised as a named designer in this 1942 collection of historicizing childrenswear for Saks Fifth Avenue. Saks Fifth Avenue. Advertisement. September 1942.

Wilkens did not sew the garments she designed for Hollywood's elite children, instead hiring a seamstress to make the dresses she sketched for the children's clothes diaries. The technical work of draping, cutting, and sewing was not Wilkens's strength—she may never have learned to do any of these—but she knew enough to team with people who could bring her vision to life.[46]

The apex of Wilkens's Hollywood period came when her young celebrity clients wore her clothes for a Hollywood Guild charity fashion show. In the media coverage of the fashion show, Wilkens was cited as "The Moppets' Schiaparelli"—an encouraging comparison for a beginning designer. The media coverage of this fashion show also apparently caught the attention of some New York stores, which were interested in enlisting Wilkens for her talents.[47]

Not long afterward, Wilkens returned to New York, where she spent

Figure 8. Four-year-old Nancy Drury, the 1947 March of Dimes Polio Poster Girl, wore an Emily Wilkens wardrobe, including this blue coat and beret with red pom-poms and matching red mittens, for her official duties. She is pictured here with March of Dimes representative Cornelia Otis Skinner, an actress and author, 14 January 1947. Photographer unknown. Author's collection.

at least two years working for a juniors manufacturer but also occasionally designed special children's collections for Saks Fifth Avenue.[48] For example, a Saks Fifth Avenue advertisement from September 1942 (Fig. 7) describes a new collection of girls' dresses "in sizes for both big and little sister" designed by Wilkens: "Inspired by actual children's dresses of the 1850s from the Museum of Costume Art . . . but completely modern, completely practical (thanks to their gifted designer, Emily Wilkins [sic]) . . . yet preserving the lovable, small grown-up air of their century-old originals."[49] The advertisement shows six looks, with fashion illustrations of the historical inspiration side-by-side with Wilkens's new interpretation. The adaptations incorporate nineteenth-century-style trims, such as soutache braid or frog fasteners, onto 1940s silhouettes, which are much shorter and simpler in cut. Look number four has a pinafore—an element that Wilkens would later utilize in many of her playsuit ensembles.

There are two especially significant points to note in this childrenswear advertisement, which shows nascent elements of the Emily Wilkens signature style already in place. First, Wilkens is already being marketed by name as a "gifted designer;" she has already been recognized as a named designer by a major, upscale store. Second, she has already developed the museum-researched, history-inspired style for which she will later be acclaimed. However, one key element of the Emily Wilkens Young Originals concept is still missing: in the dresses for Saks, Wilkens is designing identical clothes for little girls' sizes four to six and for older girls sizes seven to fourteen. The distinctiveness of the Emily Wilkens Young Originals line would occur when Wilkens realized that the teen consumer "certainly doesn't want the same dresses she wore five years earlier, in a larger size."[50] When Wilkens branched out into her own line, she would change her designs for teen girls, recognizing that their style and fit needs are different from those of the four-year-old sister.

Even after launching her own teen-size line, Wilkens would continue to take on special childrenswear projects, such as designing a custom wardrobe for the 1947 March of Dimes polio poster girl, a blonde four-year-old named Nancy Drury. The wardrobe included "a blue coat and hat, adorned with red pompons to match her mittens. . . ."[51] (Fig. 8).

Wilkens's fashion art and her childrenswear designs both had charm, and she probably could have continued a career in either of these areas with success. But she was soon to turn her hand to a new area of design specialization—clothing for teenagers—and with this new focus she would gain nationwide recognition.

THE PLAYBILL

FOR THE LYCEUM THEATRE

Figure 9. *Junior Miss* playbill cover showing Emily Wilkens's Best & Co. designs for the female teenage characters. Left to right: Joan Newton as Lois Graves, Philip Ober as Harry Graves, Barbara Robbins as Grace Graves, Lenore Lonergan as Fuffy Adams, and Patricia Peardon as Judy Graves. Week beginning 18 October 1942. Author's collection.

Some of Emily Wilkens's most significant early designs for teenagers were actually theater costumes for the Broadway play *Junior Miss*, which opened at the Lyceum Theatre in New York City on November 18, 1941[1] (Fig. 9). *Junior Miss* was based on Sally Benson's short stories about precocious teenage girls, which had appeared in the *New Yorker*, and her 1939 novel of the same name.[2] The novel was then adapted for the stage by Jerome Chodorov and Joseph Fields.[3] *Junior Miss* was such a popular success it inspired a confectionary tribute—Junior Mints candies, introduced in 1949 and still available today, were named after the show.[4] The stage version of *Junior Miss* opened less than three weeks before the Japanese bombing of Pearl Harbor on December 7 ushered the United States into World War II.[5]

Unlike many plays today, in which the name of the costume designer figures prominently even if he or she "shopped" the costumes for a production utilizing ready-to-wear, the *Junior Miss* credits list only a wardrobe supervisor and the names of stores that provided the garments. Individual retail credits are given for the different actors: for example, Saks Fifth Avenue and Bergdorf Goodman provided the garments for Barbara Robbins, who played the mother, while the teenagers' costumes are credited to Best & Co.[6] Best & Co. was an early—if not the first—entrant into the field of specifically teen-sized fashion.[7] Since Wilkens stated that she designed the teen-agers' costumes for *Junior Miss*, she must have done so under the auspices of Best & Co.'s teen-sized line.[8]

Despite the fact that Wilkens was not listed in the opening-night production credits, the costume design job was a turning point in her career.[9] Wilkens would later acknowledge that her theater costuming efforts inspired her to create her own line of clothing that approached teenagers' clothing problems in terms of sizing, fit, and age-appropriateness.[10] Wilkens wrote in 1948, "I designed the clothes for the Broadway play, *Junior Miss*, and later for *Dear Ruth*—both plays about modern teen-agers and their problems. This was so much fun that I tackled the teen-age fashion problem in earnest."[11]

What was this "teen-age fashion problem"? Perhaps we should ask first—who *was* the teenager?

THE RISE OF THE TEENAGER

In the second decade of the twenty-first century, the concept of the teenager is so enmeshed in the collective American psyche that it is hard to realize that one hundred years earlier the designation did not yet exist.

At the turn of the twentieth century, rich young white women were either classed as "little girls" still within the realm of childhood or as debutantes ready to be married off as quickly and advantageously as possible. In Mary Roberts Rinehart's World War I–era novel *Bab: A Sub-Deb*, seventeen-year-old protagonist Barbara chafes against the strict rules for sub-debs that limit her social activities, dictate her clothing styles, and even keep her bedroom décor infantile.[12] Barbara bitterly records, " 'I'm seventeen, but I shall be a mere Child until I come out . . . One day I am a Child in the nursery . . . And the next I'm grown up and ready to be sold to the highest Bider [*sic*].' "[13] The passage to adulthood was abrupt, marked by the social ritual of the debut into society. Similarly, Nancy Mitford wrote, "no sooner did Aunt Sadie's girls show their noses outside the schoolroom than they were snapped up and married," describing her aristocratic characters' swift progression from childhood to debut to marriage and the full responsibilities of adult life in the interwar period in England.[14]

Before the status of teenager could come into being, the developmental theory of adolescence would have to change the way people thought about young women. The twentieth-century concept of adolescence is often attributed to psychologist G. Stanley Hall, who in 1904 mapped out the adolescent developmental stage as, in the words of historian Kelly Schrum, "a distinct period of crisis and preparation for life."[15] In 1945, *Parents'* magazine explained its view of adolescence: "Every person must struggle to reach and maintain some sort of workable balance between himself as an individual . . . and himself as a member of society . . . Adolescence is the period when this struggle is at its peak."[16]

Adolescence was usually defined as an age-based period from the years thirteen to eighteen, although Hall may have originally envisioned a broader definition of adolescence that included people in their early twenties.[17] The ages ending in "teen" became a special, in-between time, past childhood but not yet to full adulthood. This idea of a transitional period of life allowed young women in particular to begin experimenting with freedoms unheard of previously. By 1946, even etiquette authority Emily Post conceded that respectable girls might go out in public unchaperoned.[18] As acceptance of the adolescence theory became widespread in the first half of the twentieth century, rather than girlhood leading abruptly to matrimony, the teenage years came between them, and the concurrent growth of high schools provided a place for teenagers to mature and develop as people.[19] *Calling All Girls* magazine's columnist Alice Barr Grayson wrote in 1944, "Today's daughters and sons were born into a culture which for a long time has adhered to the principle that infancy should be prolonged—that the adolescent years, for example, should be devoted largely to getting ready for living—socially, biologically."[20]

In examining the meaning of "teenager" or "adolescent" as understood in the 1940s, we should also consider how this concept differs from current ideas. The transitional stage of adolescence accepted in the 1940s was a fairly brief period of life. In recent years, developmental psychologists such as Jeffrey Arnett have argued for a new category of "emergent adulthood" (often termed "extended adolescence" in the popular press), which pushes the boundaries for the transitional, in-between stage of life upward through the twenties.[21] Emergent adulthood is thought to be a product of globalization and technological change, with young people continuing their studies longer and postponing the traditional markers of adulthood such as marriage and parenthood.[22] Therefore, it is important to note that the teenager of the 1940s, while in a transitional stage, was much closer to entering adulthood than the teenager of the same age in the 2010s.

At the same time, adolescence today infringes downward into age ranges once securely within the bounds of childhood, both through media sexualization of children and the phenomenon of girls reaching physical puberty at increasingly younger ages.[23] In 2010, the following newspaper headline appeared: "Clothing fit for a tween: Stylish apparel, without being too grown up."[24] The article was about Canadian retailer Elena Grant offering more modest, less sexualized clothing in girls' sizes 7–14. Grant said, "It's really an untapped market in terms of retailers and designers . . . They seem to want girls to go from size 4–6x to dressing like they're on the way to the club."[25] Concern about appropriate clothing for girls at a transitional stage, and the need for designers and retailers to offer outfits that appeal both to mothers and daughters, is nothing new—nearly seventy years ago these same needs were addressed in the teen-size fashions created by Wilkens for her Emily Wilkens Young Originals line, targeting the independence-minded, white, middle-class teenager. Tellingly, in the 1940s it was the girl of thirteen who was considered too young for more sophisticated juniors clothing, while articles addressing similar issues in the early twenty-first century are more likely to focus on girls still in elementary school. While the teenager of the 1940s was closer to becoming an adult, she was also less far removed from childhood than today's teenager, who has already stepped through the preliminary stage of "tween."

Retail marketers of the 1940s struggled to conceptualize the category of teenager as a mix of age brackets and pop psychology. In 1944, an article called "Take Time for Teens," which appeared in the fashion-industry magazine *Women's Reporter*, defined the teenager in this way for its retailing audience:

> [t]he teen-ager is the adolescent girl between the ages of ten and fifteen. She is struggling to emerge from the amorphous state of childhood to the glamour of womanhood. Physically she is between child and woman; like a gawky lump of feminine awkwardness . . . Psychologically, she's a mass of churning conflicts . . . She bitterly resents being called or treated as a little girl and shows this resentment most keenly in the matter of clothes.[26]

The teenager is gendered female from the retailers' standpoint; her awkwardness and confusion create both problem and potential for those involved in the fashion industry. The "Take Time for Teens" article points to one of the corollaries of separate teenage status within our capitalist society—recognition as a potential consumer.

Sociologist Daniel Thomas Cook's work on childhood and consumer society speaks to the issues of agency and the teenage consumer. In his book *The Commodification of Childhood*, Cook ties recognition of the child consumer to an increase in children's agency and society's acceptance of their personhood.[27] Cook defines agency this way: "Agency here carries the dual meaning of acting in the name of another (serving as an agent for) and exercising a certain measure of volition (being an agent of)."[28]

Much of the rhetoric surrounding the child consumer follows the basic idea that marketing targeting children is either empowering or exploitative, but Cook argues that the child consumer is already involved in market relations even before birth.[29] Historian Kelly Schrum argues that teenage girls were both empowered and exploited by the increased attention they received once they were identified as consumers.[30]

In this book, while acknowledging the exploitative aspect of fashion marketing that trades on a young woman's insecurities about her appearance, I will show that Wilkens's teen-sized Young Originals fashions were primarily empowering to a generation of teenage girls already steeped in marketing messages regarding fashion and beauty, and Wilkens's presence as a youthful named designer was inspirational to young women exerting agency in a consumer society.

Schrum argues that the "assumption that all girls had some figure problem to be controlled was at the core of teenage girls' consumer culture."[31] This idea is certainly central to Wilkens's work and is part of what Wilkens was referring to when she wrote of addressing the "teen-age fashion problem." However, the physical challenges of an adolescent figure were only part of the concern; Wilkens's designs were also intended to help teenagers navigate social and cultural challenges attendant on their status between childhood and adulthood.

JUNIOR MISS AND THE STATE OF TEENAGE FASHION IN THE EARLY 1940S

In order to understand the context in which Wilkens's designs for teenagers evolved and to appreciate what the Emily Wilkens Young Originals line would accomplish, it is also helpful to understand the state of teenage fashion when she entered the field—what American teen girls were wearing in the early 1940s. Sally Benson's novel (an adaptation of her short stories) *Junior Miss*, upon which the play was based, offers a useful, if fictional, case study.[32]

The novel introduces twelve-year-old New Yorker Judy Graves and her fashion issues in the first chapter, in which Judy falls in love with an autumn "leaf red" wool tweed coat with a "dashing squirrel collar which buttons snugly under the chin . . ."[33] The coat comes in girls' sizes 7–14, which at age twelve Judy would be expected to fit.[34] Judy needs a new coat, and while the novel never even raises the possibility of Upper-East-Sider Judy going down to Thirty-Eighth Street alone to make the purchase, her mother is willing to take her shopping the next weekend and let her try on her selection.

The problem is with Judy's figure. Judy's slim fifteen-year-old sister, Lois, speaking in the voice of teenage peers by whom Judy will be judged, says Judy would look "pregnant" or like "a sack of meal" in the belted coat and pronounces, "Judy shouldn't wear a belt, especially a belt with a *bow*. She'll be excruciating in it."[35] Benson describes Judy's figure: "She was tall for her twelve years and heavily built. From her shoulders to her knees she was entirely shapeless, which gave her a square, broad look in spite of her height."[36] As a result, Judy's little-girls' size clothes do not fit properly. "Her dress, a soft-blue one, smocked at the sleeves, was supposed to hang gracefully from the shoulders in straight folds, but instead it pulled as though she had been stuffed into it."[37] Preparing costumes for this character must have struck a personal chord for Wilkens, again recalling her own experience of a "pudgy teenage waistline under a bunchy 'kid's dress."[38] Judy's efforts to transform her body into the fashionable ideal by sucking in her stomach and skipping lunch must have spoken to Wilkens as well—in her later books she would offer healthier alternatives for creating a more slender look through exercise and nutritious eating.[39]

Judy's efforts at self-improvement are not effective, and when she finally does get to the little girls' coat department to try on the coat of her dreams, the "sleekly elegant" salesclerk is dubious about whether it will fit.[40] The clerk is correct; the coat is too tight: "I'm afraid she's a little large for a fourteen."[41] She suggests that Judy try the junior-miss department, but here is the real difficulty for Judy and girls like her—they really fall somewhere in between. Judy is too large for the little girls' sizes, but her figure is not developed enough for the juniors' department. Society had changed to acknowledge the teenager as a new category needing styles that were neither childlike nor fully adult, but ready-to-wear had not yet caught up. There are no specific teenage clothes for Judy to purchase, and the store's available merchandise is inappropriate in both fit and styling. While it seems perfectly acceptable for older sister Lois to already look "like a delicate miniature of her mother," Lois decrees, "it's perfectly silly to think that Judy could wear a junior-miss coat. It would be too old for her. You don't want her to look like her own grandmother, do you?"[42] Not only is the juniors sizing wrong for Judy's figure, but fashion etiquette argues against Judy's adopting a look that might be considered too mature or sophisticated. At the end of the chapter, Lois champions her sister, helping Judy squash herself into the ill-fitting coat and ultimately convincing their mother to buy it.

The solution Benson offers for the fictional Judy is that she exert agency to choose her own clothing, despite practical concerns and the rational reservations of her mother. But Wilkens must have seen Judy's fashion dilemma as a more widespread problem, and she immediately began inwardly formulating design solutions.

The first challenge is one of silhouette—if, indeed, belts with bows draw attention to a waistline in a negative way, what could work better? For a theater-costume designer creating garments for a specific actress in a specific role, it is simple enough to work a transformation of character by improving the character's wardrobe. And in fact, as long as the majority of American girls were having their own clothes custom-made (whether by a professional dressmaker or at home) silhouette choice and correct fit would have been the primary challenges for making the young teen figure look its best.

However, once ready-to-wear clothing with its limited range of sizes is generally available and worn, Judy's problem of being between a little-girlish and a womanly figure becomes much greater. Lois says scornfully, "Anybody would think . . . that nobody had ever heard of alterations in this family."[43] However, a ready-to-wear garment can only be altered so much, especially when it is too small in places. Even as Wilkens formulated an individual solution for the character of Judy, she also must have pondered a mass-market solution that would provide other young teen girls with clothing that actually fit their figures, as well as enabling them to exert agency by expressing their personal taste and identity through their wardrobes.

It was generally accepted in the 1940s that a tailored dress or sweater-and-skirt ensemble was appropriate as school clothing for teenage girls.[44] One advice author noted, "The freedom and durability of sweaters and skirts will always assure their popularity for school wear."[45] In the 1930s, the casual style of bare legs and ankle socks had moved from the school gymnasium into the classroom, as sweater-and-skirt ensembles were increasingly paired with ankle socks and saddle shoes.[46]

At least part of the appeal of this look must have been the minimal undergarments it required. In 1935, a survey of female college students revealed that most of them wore as their standard underpinnings just a bra, a two-way stretch girdle with panty (or a simplified panty girdle), and a silk slip. The National Retail Dry Goods Association noted that the slip was reserved for sheer dresses, and "with the ubiquitous campus uniform of sweater and skirt no slip is considered necessary."[47] The skirt-and-sweater ensemble also allowed young women to eliminate cumbersome legwear. In these years before the introduction of tights or pantyhose, the standard in full leg coverings was a complicated system of delicate stockings suspended from garters—it is no wonder that young women preferred the comfort and ease of bare legs and ankle socks, which came to be known as "bobby socks."

Bobby socks were not an item made specifically for teenagers—the same item of hosiery might be sold to an adult woman for home or factory work wear and would simply be called an "anklet," the term preferred by the National Association of Hosiery Mills. Only when worn by a teenager in the distinctive sweater-skirt-anklet combination did the socks become "bobby socks."[48] This teenage look was so pervasive that it gave rise in the 1940s to the term "bobby-soxer" as a synonym for teenage girl.[49]

Jennifer M. Mower and Elaine L. Pedersen, in a study of women's clothing consumption during World War II, described their findings: "After completing a number of interviews, we realized that many of the women we interviewed recalled wearing skirts and sweaters but not much else."[50] Twenty-seven of the thirty women that Mower and Pedersen interviewed for their study were in school for at least part of the war period, and eighteen of their respondents "remembered wearing pleated wool skirts—Pendleton plaid, if you could afford it—with blouses and sweaters; and bobby socks with saddle shoes or penny loafers."[51] Mower and Pedersen came to realize that their respondents' consistent answers reflected the ubiquity of the bobby-soxer style among teenagers; the authors concluded that their respondents' experiences as consumers during World War II were probably similar to those of teenagers throughout the United States.[52]

A sixteen-year-old girl writing in to *Parents'* magazine's "Problems: Teenage" problem-solving column in 1945 recounted asking her thirteen-year-old sister why the younger sister was always borrowing the older girl's clothes: "Her reply was that her own were too babyish. It was true. Her cotton dresses did not fit in at all with all her schoolmates' skirts and sweaters. I told mother so and now that she's buying Babs' clothes like the rest of her gang's, I don't have any trouble."[53] The sweater and skirt was one way of negotiating the teen fashion problem, as the look was socially approved as age-appropriate, and the stretch of knits reduced fit problems.

However, the key to adult approval of the sweater-and-skirt ensemble still lay in the fit of the garments. Tightly fitting sweaters might make a girl look too sexy, which was clearly deemed inappropriate.[54] At the other extreme, teenage girls in the first half of the 1940s often wore their sweaters in a very baggy style called the Sloppy Joe, which did not conform to adults' concerns with neatness in appearance. The extra fullness equaled "sloppy," which was thought to show a laziness not just with respect to dress but also of intellect and even morality, while the "Joe" indicates an appropriation of menswear. Women's studies scholar Georganne Scheiner, in a discussion of the 1945 film version of *Junior Miss* (costumed by Bonnie Cashin rather than by Wilkens), places the sweater-and-skirt ensembles worn by Judy and her friend Fuffy within the parameters of "standard bobby-soxer garb" and notes that, "[t]here was a certain subversiveness in the style of the middle-class bobby-soxer . . . [a]lthough these style practices may seem superficial and far from the politics of resistance. . . ."[55] Wilkens would later admonish teenagers that a job-seeker with poor grooming, attired in a baggy sweater and ankle socks, "seldom gets a chance to show what she can do. Her untidy appearance tells me that she is careless, probably shirks work, and hasn't the ambition to keep herself well groomed."[56]

Wilkens's theater costumes for *Junior Miss*'s protagonist Judy (thirteen years old in the stage version) move her from typical sweater, skirt, and

Figure 10. Patricia Peardon, John Cushman, Billy Redfield, Lenore Lonergan in *Junior Miss*. Photograph by Lucas-Pritchard. Reproduced by permission of the Museum of the City of New York.

ankle socks in Act 1, Scene One, to a progressively more polished look, culminating in eveningwear in the final scene—mirroring Judy's growth as a character, but also reflecting Wilkens's developing ideas about teenage fashions. Wilkens's costume designs for the stage version of *Junior Miss* included a plaid jumper with lederhosen-like suspenders worn over a light-colored sweater for Judy and a pleated skirt in a different tartan, also worn with a light-colored sweater, for Fuffy[57] (Fig. 10). Both girls pair their sweater ensembles with ankle socks and penny loafers—a typical bare-legged bobby-soxer look. This photo probably shows the actresses wearing the costumes for the first scenes of the play, representing the status quo in teenage girls' casual wear.

Judy and Fuffy's unflattering sweater-and-skirt ensembles are contrasted with a smart dress worn by big-sister Lois (Fig. 9). The double-breasted bodice of Lois's dress is reminiscent of nineteenth-century military uniforms, such as those of the American Civil War. The menswear-inspired bodice is contrasted with a feminine, full, dirndl skirt. To frame the costumes in terms popularized by *Glamour* magazine, Lois' dress would have been a "do," and Judy and Fuffy's outfits would have been a "don't," according to Wilkens.

Wilkens's costume designs for *Junior Miss* protagonist Judy also included a dark jumper worn over a neat, light-colored blouse with puffed sleeves—a look that anticipates the signature Emily Wilkens Young Originals style.[58] This is a look later in the play, which shows the type of clothing that Wilkens believed to be more flattering.

Another 1940s teen fashion trend reflected in the *Junior Miss* book, script, and theater costuming was the charm bracelet. Multiple charm bracelets could be worn at once—Benson's *Junior Miss* mentions Judy's two charm bracelets, and the script adaptation calls for Judy's character to wear three brassy charm bracelets in the opening act.[59] A publicity photo for the play shows Fuffy wearing a do-it-yourself charm-style bracelet of homemade blanket-stitched baubles (Fig. 10). Some charm bracelets could be acquired already loaded with a set of charms—in the novel, Judy receives a new charm bracelet with fourteen charms, including an ice pick, tongs, lantern, and wheelbarrow, for Christmas. In sophisticated teen fashion, Judy tells Fuffy, "'Daddy picked it out all by himself,' . . . There was pride in her voice, as though she were speaking of a backward child who had suddenly and amazingly refused to fit a square peg into a round hole."[60] This is the voice of the fashion-savvy teen sophisticate, who is shocked to find a parent—especially a father—who is able to keep up.

Wilkens herself wore a charm bracelet, just as her young clients did. On October 11, 1946, a small notice appeared in the lost-and-found section of the *New York Times* classifieds: "Gold four leaf clover charm; midtown; sentimental; reward. Emily Wilkens, 519 8 Av. BR 9-3336."[61] She had somehow lost one of the charms from her bracelet, clearly one that held sentimental, if not monetary, value.[62]

Seventeen magazine, which had only recently begun publication, also featured complete charm bracelets. A charm bracelet graced the cover of *Seventeen*'s third issue in November 1944.[63] A 1947 issue contains two advertisements for charms and charm bracelets from different manufacturers. One charm bracelet of "eyeful trifles" attempts to indoctrinate the homemaker of tomorrow with brand loyalty today, in a piece of jewelry featuring miniatures of trademarked goods such as Crisco shortening, Shredded Ralston breakfast cereal, Pepsi cola, and Mobil oil.[64] The wearer is literally chained to the products. *Seventeen*'s own promotions department encouraged potential advertisers to view teenage readers as impressionable with regard to brands and to view an investment in advertising to these teens as one that might result in the dividend of later brand loyalty.[65]

Other charms might be added individually, and might include items not originally intended for girls' charm bracelets. Judy adds to one of her charm bracelets a tiny gold baseball that commemorated her father's 1916 baseball championship.[66]

Perhaps Wilkens's four-leaf clover charm was one of the type added individually, since it had enough sentimental value for her to offer a reward. And did she ever get it back? That remains a mystery.

Charm bracelets would remain a popular fashion accessory into the 1950s; juniors designer Anne Fogarty was still listing noisy charm bracelets in the theater as one of her pet peeves in 1959![67]

For Wilkens, costuming the female teenage characters for the Broadway production of *Junior Miss* was both an inspiration and a step toward becoming a fully fledged fashion "designer for the [t]eens."[68]

E xtrapolating from personal experience and that of the fictional Judy Graves, Emily Wilkens sought a mass-market solution to the young teenager's fashion difficulties—a solution firmly grounded in the framework of American ready-to-wear. Wilkens's significance in American fashion history centers on the unique aspects of her business, one of which was the relationship she enjoyed with the manufacturers of her garments—an association that allowed her to exert agency by retaining both fiscal and artistic control over her own label, Emily Wilkens Young Originals. Other significant elements of the business included having her own name on the garment label, establishing a fabric-supply deal with Everfast, and filing many design patents to protect her dress designs and her brand.

Wilkens's ready-to-wear career began in earnest in 1943, when she was only in her mid-twenties, by targeting her namesake line at girls ages twelve through sixteen.[1] Up until this point, most manufacturers had not been willing to invest in good design for teenage clothing. Journalist Mabel Greene, writing for the *New York Sun*, announced, "To the small list of talented creators who specialize in clothes for the sub-deb school girl should be added the name of Emily Wilkens, young designer with youthful ideas."[2] The sub-deb label was used for teenage girls below the debutante age. This old-fashioned language reflected the traditional divide between a debutante, who was "out" in society and eligible for marriage, and the girl who had not yet made her debut and therefore had a very restricted social life.

On the other hand, the terms "teen-ager," "teen," and "teen-age" were not new to the 1940s. Kelly Schrum traces these words for young people ages thirteen to eighteen to the 1920s at least and notes that they were linked to high school attendance and more often used for girls than for boys.[3] During the 1940s, the word "teenager" expressed the reality of the freedom to socialize that teen girls enjoyed: going out to the movies, to the soda shop for a Coca-Cola, or to teen clubs. Wilkens marketed her clothes as garments for "teenagers," not "sub-debs," linguistically reinforcing that her clients possess a certain level of autonomy—they already "have a life."

A 1947 *Kiplinger's Personal Finance* article, "Teenagers as Customers," identified three different categories of products for which businesses might need to make adjustments if they wished to reach the teenage market: First were products such as soft drinks, books, and records, which the author believed only needed special promotions or advertisements to appeal to teenagers. Secondly, the article cited products that might need different labels or packaging. Finally, there was the category in which the product itself might need to be changed for the teenager: "articles like underwear and dresses that must be varied specially to fit the changing figures of adolescent girls. It is this part of the field that has had the least intelligent cultivation, and in which enterprising designers, manufacturers and retailers have reaped fortunes recently."[4] In 1943, however, it was not a given in the retail world that such changes were necessary in order to sell to teenage girls. As one of those "enterprising designers" who saw the need to create clothing specifically for this age group, Wilkens seized on just the right moment to do so.

The *Kiplinger's* article cites Mary Lewis, vice president of Best & Co., as the person "popularly regarded as the originator of special teenage clothes."[5] Youthful, blonde, and curly-haired, Lewis was not a designer but a store executive in a time period when the fashion industry offered the best opportunity for American women to advance in their business careers. Of American women who held executive-level jobs by 1940, eighty-four percent were employed in the fashion industry.[6] Lewis was a merchant with an instinctive ability to sense trends—besides her involvement with teen-size clothing, she was also an early backer of Claire McCardell's monastic dress, which had a loose, waistless, bias cut and could be belted according to the wearer's taste. The monastic dress appealed to women because it met a need for flexibility in their wardrobes; the dress was a sellout hit. Mary Lewis was an apt identifier of what the customer needed.[7]

The *Kiplinger's* article then goes on to name Wilkens as the designer responsible for the teen-size concept gaining momentum.[8] Throughout her career, Wilkens had the ability to identify what was up-and-coming, and to find a way to market her own interests to capitalize on the trend. In her own label, Wilkens sought first to create clothing that was appropriately sized for the young teenage customer.

Today, American ready-to-wear sizing for women's clothes revolves around the three basic systems of juniors, misses, and plus-size garments, with additional offerings in height- and proportion-based petite and tall sizes. Clothes marketed to teenagers are generally produced in the juniors size range. In the 1940s, women's ready-to-wear manufacturers already offered several different sizing systems, from the slender figure of the junior miss, to the standard figure of misses, and the fuller figure catered to by half-sizes. *Life* magazine informed its readers in 1942, "Compared to a regular Miss, the Junior Miss has smaller and higher breasts, smaller waist, shorter distance between waist and neck, flat stomach and backside."[9] In theory each sizing system targeted a different customer, with junior-miss sizes aimed at the customer in her teens or early twenties.

However, Wilkens's costume work with *Junior Miss*, her experience working with a juniors manufacturer, and her personal experience led her to believe that existing girls' and juniors' ready-to-wear sizes did not meet the needs of most teenagers. Just as the fictional Judy Graves, too young for junior-miss sizes, struggled to find children's-size clothes that fit her properly, so did many real-life American teenagers. American society of the 1940s recognized a special status of teenagers between childhood and adulthood, but American ready-to-wear offerings did not always reflect this. Teenage customers were expected to fit into slim children's clothing until they suddenly blossomed into the sleek, hourglass figure of junior-miss-size garments. Wilkens noted the inadequacy of childrenswear for teenagers, stating that teenagers had a larger waist and hips but narrower shoulders than the standard size 10–16 girls' dress of the period.[10] At the other end of the size spectrum, Wilkens observed, "I made a survey of teen-age figures and found that they were far different from those of the

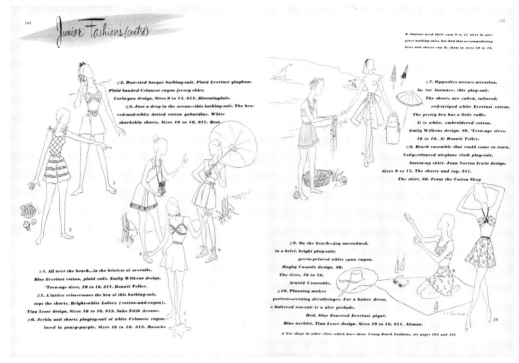

Figure 11. Sketches of beachwear by designers including Emily Wilkens and Tina Leser show three different sizing systems. The Emily Wilkens teen-sized design on the right-hand page is the bra top and shorts of the "Weekender" country club ensemble. *Vogue*, 1 June 1944, 144–145. © *Vogue*, *Condé Nast*.

accepted 'juniors.' They were shorter, thicker through the waist and hips, shaped entirely differently from the way they would be a few years later."[11]

Teen-sized clothing was meant to bridge the gap between childrenswear and juniors sizing. Teen sizes were designed to fit the teenage girl whose body was beginning to go through puberty, experiencing changes such as weight gain and breast development, but who had not yet had a "growth spurt" and become more slender. While a few stores, such as Best & Co., were already selling teen-sized garments, Wilkens believed that there was much room for improvement in the current teen-size offerings. As noted previously, her idea was to create a teen-sized line of fashionable clothing that would offer something between little girls' and juniors' styling.

When teen-sized clothing was featured in general fashion periodicals, it was often in the context of articles geared toward the older teenager—who was usually conceptualized as the junior-miss customer. In fact, there was probably some overlap. For example, in 1944 *Vogue* magazine included in its editorial coverage of "Junior Fashions" swim and play ensembles in three different sizing systems (Fig. 11). The article states, "Juniors need their own 9 to 17 sizes in one-piece bathing-suits, but find that accommodating bras and shorts can fit them in sizes 10 to 16."[12] Juniors would need their own size in one-pieces because the junior customer was supposed to have a shorter torso than the standard misses size—"accommodating" misses bra tops would presumably have been those not cut too full for the more slight junior bust. In this two-page spread the reader encounters Joan Norton Irwin designs in junior sizes 9 to 15, Tina Leser garments in misses sizes 10 to 16, and Emily Wilkens Young Originals in teen sizes 10 to16. The range of options must have been confusing. By the postwar period, Emily Wilkens Young Originals were also available in junior sizes.

In 1943, however, Wilkens was focused on creating fashions specifically in teen sizes. She began looking for opportunities to create a new line of clothes that would solve the fit and styling dilemmas represented by the character of Judy Graves.

When Wilkens took her idea of a stand-alone teen-sized fashion brand to the ready-to-wear manufacturing community, she did not meet with instant success. Manufacturers Roy and Ben Chalk, whom she had approached when she first returned to New York, set up a meeting for Wilkens to pitch her idea of a line focusing on fashion for teenage girls to ten manufacturers.[13] Six of the manufacturers rejected her proposal altogether; the other four vetoed her salary requirement of $5,000 per year.[14]

Wilkens's challenge was to sell manufacturers not just on her designs but also on the idea of the teenage girl as a consumer with a certain amount of autonomy. Sociologist Kelley Massoni writes that this process would also be key to the establishment of *Seventeen* magazine the following year; the magazine would implement a whole campaign marketing its ideal reader, Teena, to advertisers.[15]

It is important to note that the United States was deeply involved in World War II by this time, and that the Limitations Order L-85 regulation had been introduced the previous year by the War Production Board (WPB).[16] The L-85 regulation limited the fabric yardage allowed in most garments and was intended to prevent fashionable changes in silhouette,

Figure 12. L-85 Regulation before and after: "The original dress at the right uses three and seven eighths yards of thirty-nine inch width material. By eliminating the pleating above the hem (right), a half yard of 700 square inches of thirty-nine inch width material was saved in the dresses at the left, which conforms to the order." 1943. Library of Congress Prints & Photographs Division, FSA/Office of War Information Black-and-White Negatives, LC-USW35-028546-A (b&w film neg.).

which would have required adjustments of machinery and technique as well as requiring extra labor (Fig. 12). Exempt garments included wedding gowns, maternity clothes, clothing for infants and children up to age four, religious vestments, and burial shrouds.[17] Any new teen-sized line would be subject to the limits of the L-85 regulation. However, the war's impact on American fashion was still less dramatic than was the case in Britain, where clothes had been rationed since June 1941, with every garment assigned a coupon value and each individual allotted sixty-six coupons per year.[18]

Although the L-85 regulation restricted what Wilkens could create in a teen-sized line, in some ways it may have also helped highlight her work. Newness was at a premium at this time, and Wilkens's new teen approach may have seemed even more exciting and newsworthy than it would have appeared under normal circumstances. Bernice Chambers wrote, "Yet what manufacturer, in a war year of fabric shortages and government restrictions, would assume the risk of pioneering in a new field of fashion enterprise? Miss Wilkens knew that she would have to take that risk, herself; so one day, when the urge was greater than ever, she rented a small space in the corner of a workroom and started to design."[19]

It seems that the space she rented was in Roy and Ben Chalk's clothing manufacturing facility, where they were able to observe her work ethic as well as her design ideas. Wilkens's daughter, Jane Michael, recalls that Wilkens was "full of ideas and verve" and that coupled with her beauty, Wilkens had a compelling charm—she was very convincing.[20] At any rate, soon after the original round of meetings Ben Chalk changed his mind and decided to manufacture Emily Wilkens Young Originals in teen sizes 10 to 16.[21]

Wilkens created her line in partnership with the Chalk brothers. Their manufacturing business had been producing junior-sized coats under the brand name Vogue Girl Coat Co. for several years, as well as catering to another niche sizing market—what was then termed "chubby-sized" girls' clothing.[22] Manufacturer Ben Chalk was officially recognized as a leader in the women's apparel field in 1947 by the industry publication *Fashion Trades*, along with journalist Virginia Pope, retailers Stanley Marcus and Dorothy Shaver, and a host of other, less-familiar names, including fabric producers and labor leaders.[23]

Although the Chalks were well established in the garment industry, it was Emily Wilkens's name that would appear on the garment labels (Plate 4). In the twentieth century, labels became a crucial part of marketing luxury goods such as designer ready-to-wear. The concept of the label's importance is even embedded in the English word "label," which can either mean the physical tag identifying a garment's maker or a synonym for "line of garments." Wilkens's daughter, Jane Michael, recounts that the pink-and-green flower on the Emily Wilkens Young Originals label was Wilkens's own design.[24] A similar flower would appear on the label of Wilkens's designs in the early 1950s (Plate 5).

In both color and motif, the Emily Wilkens signature flower recalls interior designer Dorothy Draper's 1941 work for the Camellia House Supper Club at the Drake Hotel in Chicago. The Camellia House was elaborately themed with objects from plates to menus, paper napkins to invitations, all featuring a floral motif in a similar color scheme as Emily's garment label—camellia pink and "Empire" green, slightly deeper than the shade used by Wilkens.[25] However, Wilkens's pink flowers are more abstracted than Draper's camellias.

The color combination of pink and green was fashionable in the 1940s.

April 18, 1944. E. WILKENS Des. 137,723

DRESS

Filed Feb. 24, 1944

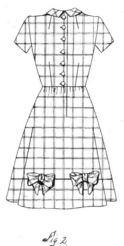

Figure 13. Emily Wilkens used design patents to protect her work from style piracy. Emily Wilkens. Design patent for a window-pane check dress. Des. 137,723. 18 April 1944.

Even the street-level walls of the revamped New York City department store Gimbels were touted as "elegantly pink and elegantly green."[26] The pink-and-green color scheme was also personal for Wilkens—around this time, she decorated her New York apartment in colors *House Beautiful* described as "moss green" and "radiant pink." Although she rented a furnished apartment, Wilkens made the space her own by adding draperies, a table skirt, and a couch cover in pink and green dress materials from the fabric collections used for her garment designs.[27] A 1949 press-release biography of Wilkens by her publicist Eleanor Lambert noted, "She loves pink and green as a combination, but usually wears navy or brown."[28] Wilkens did, however, sometimes combine the colors in her fashion designs, such as a pink-and-green strapless playsuit from 1947.[29] Wilkens would write later that some shades of green and pink could be as tranquil and soothing for a bedroom as blues and off-whites.[30] "Always remember that color can truly influence how one feels," Wilkens noted.[31] The colors for her label were chosen both for their fashion quotient and to reflect what made Wilkens, personally, happiest.

The relationship between Wilkens and the Chalks was described as a "co-operative" partnership by Bernice Chambers, who wrote: "One of the few American designers who are known as heads of their own firms is Emily Wilkens. In 1943, with a co-operative partner, she established the company, Young Originals, for the manufacture of girls' clothes."[32] (By "girls'" Chambers means teens, not little girls, as in twenty-first-century usage.) What is interesting to note about Chambers's comment is that she does not qualify this statement by saying that Wilkens is, for example, a rare twenty-something designer, or a rare female designer, or a rare new-comer to the industry. Wilkens was one of the few ready-to-wear designers in the United States empowered in both the creative and business aspects of her firm.

Being a named designer-partner rather than just an employee seems crucial to Wilkens's award-winning recognition as a designer. As a named designer she was better known both within the industry and to the general public. For example, at a January 1945 meeting of the fashion industry's Children's Wear Discussion Group on the "teen fashion revolution," Wilkens was the only woman and the only designer featured in the forum alongside a list of male manufacturers including her business partner Ben Chalk, American Debuteen's Philip Oretsky, Junior First's Harry Jaffee, and TeenTimer's Jules Rubinstein.[33]

Similarly, Wilkens was often the only teenage clothing designer named in information reaching the general public. A May 1944 *New York Times* article showcasing teen fashions, "High Jinks in Style," included her "green window-pane checked dress made of Everfast cotton," for which Wilkens had been granted a patent—Des. 137,723—in April (see discussion below for more about Wilkens's patenting of her designs)[34] (Fig. 13). Wilkens's clothes are credited, "Design by Emily Wilkens," followed by the price, and then the store, Bonwit Teller. She is the only named designer featured; other ensembles are simply credited to the respective store: Abraham & Straus, Lord & Taylor, Saks-34th St., Jane Engel, Bloomingdales, Mc-Creery's. Ironically, here even the New York–based Lord & Taylor is not associated with a designer's name, although Vice President Dorothy Shaver had been at the forefront of the movement promoting American designers by name in the store's advertising campaigns beginning in 1932.[35]

As a designer with her name on the label, Wilkens had greater opportunities for receiving credit in print media than most apparel manufacturers. Publishers differed in their policies toward granting credit in print, ranging from no credits at all (readers were expected to write in and request the credit information), to credits for retailers, to credits for manufacturers. However, some publishers believed that crediting a wholesaler was too commercial and would only credit a manufacturer if linked to the prestige of a named designer, such as a Lilly Daché hat, a glove by Isabel, or a dress by Emily Wilkens.[36]

Fashion historian Rebecca Arnold notes that in the 1930s "as a gradual shift towards personality-driven promotional techniques took hold in American fashion and national identity became a selling tool, the media began to name designers who had until then worked anonymously for stores and manufacturers."[37] Arnold writes that during World War II, the marketing of American designers took on a patriotic urgency, and industry groups such as the Fashion Group and the New York Dress Institute took up the challenge to recognize designers.[38] Publicist Eleanor Lambert, who worked with the New York Dress Institute and helped found the Coty Awards, also contributed to name recognition of American fashion designers by promoting her clients, one of whom was Wilkens.[39]

However, despite all these efforts, many if not most American ready-to-wear designers of the 1940s still worked anonymously for manufacturers, and those who did manage to get name recognition often had to share billing with the company or investor's name, such as Jo Copeland-Pattulo Modes, or Norman Norell at Traina-Norell. Norell even accepted a lower salary in exchange for naming rights.[40] This makes it extremely impressive that Wilkens as a woman of twenty-six was able to wield so much control over her name and designs.

The Emily Wilkens Young Originals business address was 519 Eighth Avenue, located between Thirty-Fifth and Thirty-Sixth Streets in the New York City garment district.[41] The garment district, also called Seventh Avenue, continues as a center of clothing manufacturing as well as a location for showrooms on the west side of Midtown Manhattan. Placement in the garment district gave Wilkens convenient access to others in the industry as well as to essential garment-center resources such as fabric and trim. Although many American brands came to be designed in New York but made overseas, designers such as Nanette Lepore continue the tradition of New York garment-center manufacturing into the twenty-first century.

The Emily Wilkens Young Originals label was initially created in a deal with Everfast for fabric supply, a key practical component for the fledgling fashion enterprise.[42] The United States' raw silk stocks had been taken over by the government on August 27, 1941, pre-dating American entry into World War II. Rayon became more difficult for manufacturers to obtain after Pearl Harbor, and supplies of all fabrics were limited.[43] In fall 1943, when Wilkens was working to establish her Young Originals line, fabric shortages were a real threat to a company's ability to deliver orders. Wilkens's agreement with Everfast gave her unusual access to the fabric she would need. She also worked directly with the Everfast fabric house to develop colors, color combinations, and fabrics specifically for her teenage clients.[44]

According to Bernice Chambers, Everfast was defined as the "[t]rade name for [a] large group of cotton, linen and rayon fabrics, including EVERFAST suiting and uniform cloth, all of which carry guarantee of color resistance. Manufactured by Everfast Fabrics, Inc."[45] Before Wilkens even showed her first Emily Wilkens Young Originals collection, Everfast ran advertising with this testimonial from Wilkens: "This is my first big collection of teen-age play clothes, and I have featured cotton and rayon fabrics by Everfast. Not only was I inspired by these wonderful fabrics, but I have worked on them knowing that they will always retain their original sparkling colors after numerous washings."[46]

As indicated in this ad, a significant feature of the Everfast garments was their washability; in 1940s parlance, they were "tubbable."[47] As the name implied, they would not fade in the wash. Ease of fabric care was a significant factor in marketing to the teen demographic. One home-economics textbook cautioned high school girls:

> Perhaps you have had the experience of buying material without considering whether or not it would soil quickly or could be cleaned easily. A material that requires cleaning often, or is difficult to clean, is more expensive at the same price than one that does not soil easily, since the cost of frequent cleanings or launderings should be added

Figure 14. Spring/Summer 1945 "Flutterbye" ensemble of Everfast cotton (right), shown with solid pinafore layered over gray and white striped playsuit. Photograph by Eileen Darby. © Eileen Darby Images, Inc.

to the original cost . . . When purchasing material, ask yourself these questions: Will it need to be pressed often? Will water spot it? Can it be cleaned successfully?[48]

The July and August 1944 edition of *Cotton News* praised Wilkens's most recent collection for its ease of care, noting that one of the collection's selling points was that a teenage girl could launder and iron the garments for herself.[49]

Wilkens continued to be a proponent of cotton as a year-round (not just for spring and summer) fashion fabric. In 1946, Wilkens spoke at the seventh annual Cotton Research Congress in Dallas, suggesting that the cotton industry work to create greater variety in cotton fabric construction, improve wrinkle resistance, and offer a year-round "cotton story" with the addition of more "winter cottons." She showed the Cotton Research Congress her own quilted cotton ensemble, with floor-length skirt and leg-o-mutton sleeves, inspired by the 1890s.[50]

Many of Wilkens's 1940s designs, particularly for play clothes, were created using Everfast cottons; these are the designs for which she is best known, as some of them have been exhibited. "Flutterbye" was a 1945 Spring/Summer ensemble of striped Everfast cotton playsuit with a coordinating pinafore that could be worn over it (Fig. 14).[51] The playsuit was shown in the 1998 Costume Institute at the Metropolitan Museum of Art exhibition *American Ingenuity: Sportswear 1930s–1970s*. The complete ensemble is now in the collection of Parsons, the New School.

The catalogue from *American Ingenuity*, curated by Richard Martin, includes a publicity photo of one of Wilkens's designs, and the caption labels the dress "Sunmere."[52] The dress in the publicity photo is actually the "Flutterbye" playsuit and pinafore ensemble of Everfast cotton discussed above. "Sunmere" was a brand name for Everfast rayon rather than the name of a dress model.

From her first Emily Wilkens Young Originals collection for Spring/ Summer 1944, Wilkens would incorporate Everfast's rayon fabrics as well. Her 1944 designs included a washable rayon called Erin cloth used, for example, in a blouse with a cotton pinafore over it.[53]

A full-color advertisement in *Harper's Bazaar* in 1945 (Plate 6) showed a teenage girl in a pink version of an Emily Wilkens dress and was meant to promote both the new rayon fabric and the designer:

> Portrait of a young girl in a postwar fabric—'Sunmere' by Everfast is the first of the miracle fabrics. Woven by Ponemah Mills of 1.0 denier rayon, it is silken in texture and as easy to wash and iron as all fabrics by Everfast. Emily Wilkens has styled it for teen-agers in a group of dresses in copen, turquoise, pink or maize, to be found exclusively at Bonwit Teller in New York. About $23.[54]

Here, the advertisement makes a point to tell the reader that "Sunmere" is woven from 1.0 denier rayon yarns. Denier expresses the fineness of a yarn as a measurement of weight per length (.05 gram weights per standard 450-meter skein). In the 1940s the coarsest rayon yarns produced were 900 denier, while 1 denier such as that used in Sunmere was the finest available.[55] As with many other industries, the American textile industry continued to advertise and promote its goods during the war, assuring the public that after victory new and exciting products would be available to the public. Everfast had introduced Sunmere fabric at a

Figure 15. Emily Wilkens
in her Botany wool suit
appearing at the Gotham
Hosiery Company spring
1945 hosiery fashion
show. She is pictured with
a "portrait marionette"
in matching ensemble.
Author's collection.

fashion show at the Plaza Hotel in New York in November of 1944, as
one of two new "postwar" materials (meaning not widely commercially
available until wartime restrictions were lifted in late 1945) of super-fine
rayon yarns that they had developed. Journalist Virginia Pope wrote that
Sunmere "looks and feels like silk."[56]

Ponemah Mills, where the Sunmere rayon used in Wilkens's 1945 designs was woven, had been operating in the town of Taftville, Connecticut,
since the late nineteenth century.[57] Construction of the mill, situated on
the Shetucket River north of Norwich and approximately forty miles from
Wilkens's hometown of Hartford, was completed in 1871 by James S. At-
wood and Edward Taft, who gave his name to the village of Taftville.[58] The
available waterpower at this site meant that Ponemah Mills was capable of
tremendous output; when new, this mill was the largest building for the
production of cotton goods in the United States.[59]

Figure 16. Milliken Woolens featured Emily Wilkens's photograph in their advertising to teenage consumers. Milliken Woolens. Advertisement. *Seventeen*, Feb. 1947, 6.

In the first half of the twentieth century, much of the United States' cotton fabric production began to move to the South, where labor costs were lower.[60] Southern states also had the raw material for cotton production locally available, but in the area of synthetics and woolens, the South did not have an advantage of location.[61] That Ponemah Mills had converted part of its manufacturing capacity to spinning and weaving a synthetic fiber like rayon was probably a factor in its continued competitiveness and survival.

New England mills also tried to market their goods as superior in quality to southern-made goods. The Ponemah Mills ad using the Emily Wilkens design emphasizes its fabric quality with the slogan "Through a ring—the sign of a fine fabric" and the image of fabric being pulled through a woman's ring. Wilkens may have intentionally supported local New England industry through her designs, but the consideration above all was a matter of fabric availability.

Wilkens also worked with wool, at least by 1945.[62] A suit comprised of checked blouse and solid yellow skirt, shown in *Harper's Bazaar* in March of 1945, is described as Botany wool. Taking its name from Botany Bay, Australia, today Botany wool may be Australian merino, but the name is also applied to fine wool worldwide. In the 1940s, Botany was also an American brand name for wool from Botany Worsted Mills of Passaic, New Jersey, which is probably what the *Harper's* reference denoted.[63] Wilkens herself wore this wool suit in a different colorway with a lime green skirt at Gotham Hosiery Company's spring hosiery fashion show in February 1945 (Fig. 15). A Milliken wool advertisement from 1947 shows that by the late forties Wilkens had forged a fabric alliance with Milliken Woolens (Fig. 16).[64]

Apparently Wilkens was concerned about the impact of copycats on her business, because in February 1944 she began applying for design patents to protect many of her original dress models. Wilkens applied for, and received, the patents in her own name, rather than allowing her company to own the patents. The patent documents contain a technical rendering of the garment being patented, and refer to the invention as "a new, original, and ornamental Design for a Dress."[65]

Fashion designers in the United States had been grappling with the problem of copying, or style piracy, for some years (and it remains a contentious issue). A manufacturer-created system penalizing stores that

Figure 17. This "young black" dress from the first collection of Emily Wilkens Young Originals was featured in advertising and received widespread media coverage. Emily Wilkens. Design patent for a "young black" dress with removable jerkin. Des. 137,566. 28 March 1944.

bought copies was struck down under the Sherman Anti-Trust Act in 1941.[66] By filing for patent protection, Wilkens was making an effort to protect her original designs by working within existing intellectual property law. Design patents allowed mid-century American fashion designers to register and patent a new and original design and offered legal protection from copying for three-and-a-half years plus a possible extension of time upon request.[67] Sportswear designs made up the greatest percentage of patent applications for clothing.[68] However, even commentators of the era argued that the process was "both expensive and cumbersome. As a technique, it is too slow for so swiftly paced a business as the fashion industry, though it is used to some extent."[69]

Nevertheless, Wilkens filed for many design patents in her early career, and advertising aimed at other members of the fashion industry listed this patent protection as one of the factors lending exclusivity to the brand.[70] One of her first patents was for a "young black" dress (Fig. 17).[71] Another patent was filed for her teacup-motif dress, described in an advertisement

March 28, 1944.   E. WILKENS   Des. 137,563
DRESS
Filed Feb. 24, 1944

Figure 18. In the 1940s, a Coke at the drug store was a modern teenage mode of consuming caffeine, and the motif of the "teacup dress" was whimsically nostalgic. Emily Wilkens. Design patent for a dress. Des. 137,563. 28 March 1944.

as a "Tea cup dress. Pinafore in beige Erin, a washable Everfast spun rayon, 13.95. Everfast broadcloth blouse, 5.95" (Fig. 18).[72]

A dress from Wilkens's Spring/Summer 1946 collection shows the interesting journey of a Wilkens design from inspiration to patent to production. The Brooklyn Museum's Fashion and Costume Sketch Collection contains Wilkens's original sketch for this light-brown dress with an inverted triangle of smocking on the bodice (Plate 7). This smocking allows ease for expanding waistlines, and at the same time the triangular shape visually emphasizes the bust while making the waist appear smaller.

Wilkens had been pondering the English farmer's smock in the fall of 1945. For the *New York Times*'s "Fashions of the *Times*" production of October 1945, celebrating museum-object-inspired design, Wilkens created smock adaptations that were worn by fifteen women modeling the milliners' contributions to the show. The smocks formed a neutral and uniform

April 16, 1946.   E. WILKENS   Des. 144,473

DRESS

Filed Dec. 5, 1945

Figure 19. The sleeves and neckline in the technical rendering of this dress differ from those shown in an original sketch of a similar dress, in the collection of the Brooklyn Museum. Emily Wilkens. Design patent for a smocked dress. Des. 144,473. 16 April 1946.

backdrop to display the new hat designs (which the models wore), and the museum pieces that inspired the adaptations (each model carrying in her hands the object of inspiration for her hat).[73]

Wilkens continued reworking this pastoral theme as she designed her Spring/Summer 1946 collection, sketching the brown smocked dress, and then filing for a design patent on December 5, 1945. Wilkens received design patent Des. 144,473 for a slightly modified version of this dress with an open, collared neckline rather than the turtleneck shown in the sketch (Fig. 19). A clipping of a photograph, now in the Fairchild Archive's Emily Wilkens scrapbook, shows that the dress was produced in essentially the form of the original sketch, with perhaps a bit more fullness in the sleeves (which were also smocked at the wrist), and the caption of the photo informs readers of the garment's peasant-inspired origins.[74]

After World War II, as restrictions on clothing design were slowly lifted, the patent office was inundated with applications.[75] It is significant that Wilkens felt her designs were original and compelling enough to warrant patent protection, even during the years of wartime regulation.

In the weeks leading up to the unveiling of the new Emily Wilkens Young Originals line, Wilkens and the Chalks began taking out large advertisements in *Women's Wear Daily* promoting their new project.[76] On March 28, 1944, Wilkens held a showing of her Emily Wilkens Young Originals fashions in the new teenage department of Bonwit Teller in New York, before an audience of about sixty members of the fashion press, as well as a "jury" of mothers and daughters.[77] This first collection was praised by both the consumer focus group and the media, and Emily Wilkens Young Originals began its critically acclaimed success.[78]

Fashion begins with an ideal body, and Emily Wilkens worked from a conscious construction of her ideal. Her fashion designs of the 1940s are "modern" in that they require the body itself to be shaped through exercise and diet to fit the fashionable silhouette, rather than relying primarily on garments or undergarments to mold the body. Even in the 1950s, when Wilkens's garments included boned bodices and were intended to be worn over shaping undergarments, she still advocated exercise and diet as the primary means of fashioning the figure. Wilkens wrote, "I have some very definite ideas about what should be done to make the young American body look its best."[1] The quest for a wholesome, all-American style of beauty underlies all her work, from her 1940s dresses for teenage girls to her spa books for adults in the 1970s and 80s.

In Robert Harling's 1986 play *Steel Magnolias*, product-loving hairstylist Truvy's philosophy is that, "[t]here is no such thing as natural beauty."[2] For Wilkens, too, there was no such thing as natural beauty—if by "natural" we mean a "low-maintenance," do-nothing approach. According to Wilkens, "Beauty is usually due to 90 percent know-how and 10 percent nature."[3] The Wilkens approach to beauty was to invest time and work hard at one's appearance so as to give the impression of effortlessness. She described natural beauty as, "more than avocado facials and lemon hair rinses. It's a way of looking and feeling better by working WITH nature rather than against it."[4] Wilkens's philosophy was natural in terms of shunning the gaudy or overtly artificial, but her look was never un-done.

The Emily Wilkens "look," as described by the designer herself, was "youth, simplicity, glowing health, and smart good looks."[5] The ideal body for Wilkens was youthful, well-scrubbed and neat rather than overly made up, and kept healthy—and slim—through systematic diet and exercise. Wilkens wrote, "It's that 'washed baby' look we're after.'"[6] Her ideal of beauty was in keeping with a consistent theme promoted in the American media throughout Wilkens's formative years, an attractiveness based on "first . . . the beauty of health and enthusiasm that radiates from a vital young person. Second, it's grooming in every small personal detail—hair, skin, hands, feet. And third, it is dress. . . ."[7]

Fashion historian Rebecca Arnold, analyzing American beauty at the end of the 1930s, observes,

> *Vogue* clearly regarded cleanliness as a prerequisite of American femininity. The point was continually reinforced within this and other magazines by pictures of immaculately groomed models, all of whom embodied a white, middle-class standard of beauty. Mary Lynn Stewart has written of the commercial imperative that encouraged French women to view hygiene as a prerequisite of acceptable femininity, but it was in America that this idea was really developed and turned into an explicit issue of national, as well as gender, identity.[8]

Wilkens's concept of the ideal body seems to have fit perfectly with the fashion of the World War II era as promoted in *Vogue* magazine. The May 14, 1944, issue of *Vogue* featured fresh-faced, seventeen-year-old Tee Matthews wearing a pinafore-style sundress of "aqua Everfast cotton, piped with fuchsia braid," from the first Emily Wilkens Young Originals collection[9] (Plate 8). Wilkens received design patent Des. 137,565 for this pinafore (Fig. 20).

Matthews had recently begun a modeling career after a *Life* magazine photograph of her in a midriff-baring top and shorts proved a de facto pin-up for soldiers; her look is characteristic of the Emily Wilkens style. *Vogue* admonished its readers,

March 28, 1944.   E. WILKENS   Des. 137,565
PINAFORE
Filed Feb. 24, 1944

Figure 20. Design patent for the pinafore worn by Tee Matthews in *Vogue*. Emily Wilkens. Design patent for a pinafore-style sundress. Des. 137,565.

Actually, [Matthews] is no world-shaking beauty, but her particular brand of bright, burnished youth is a good look to the soldiers. . . . So . . . if you have been wearing heavy theatrical make-up and mahogany lipstick . . . it might be a tip for you to know that the new trend in looks is the natural look. And remember, this new look doesn't just happen. It's a matter of deliberately choosing a light, clear lipstick. Wearing your hair in a chipper way. Deliberately showing your glowing skin (and staying healthy, so that your skin will stay that way, too).[10]

This description of the path to beauty sounds as though Wilkens herself could have written it. Wilkens did not simply design clothes with an ideal type and figure in mind—she continuously promoted her ideal of the healthy, well-groomed body, urging women to take action to change their

Figure 21. The ideal body as imagined by Emily Wilkens and sketched by Erica Perl Merkling. Author's collection.

bodies to fit the ideal. Wilkens first articulated her formula for beauty in her 1948 book *Here's Looking at . . . You!*, edited by Dorothy Roe Lewis.[11] However, this ideal was not limited to her early work with teenagers. Wilkens would continue to espouse this beauty philosophy throughout her career; in fact, it would later become her primary focus.

In her advice, Wilkens places herself within a continuum of writers of prescriptive literature. As British *Vogue* editor Alison Settle does in her 1937 book *Clothes Line*, Wilkens emphasized simplicity, good taste, grooming, and apparel maintenance.[12] Wilkens was one of many American fashion designers of the period to publish autobiographies or advice literature. Wilkens's first effort was published in 1948, after Lilly Daché's (1946) but before Claire McCardell's (1956).[13] There were also many books of advice written specifically for teenagers in the 1940s, such as etiquette writer Bernice Bryant's 1944 *Future Perfect*.[14] Wilkens's first book is unique in being a work of prescriptive literature addressed to a teenage audience by an American fashion designer.

Wilkens would eventually publish three more books: *A New You: The Art of Good Grooming* (1965), *Secrets from the Super Spas* (1976), and *More Secrets from the Super Spas* (1983). These four books reveal several consistent components of Wilkens's beauty philosophy across all four decades, including personal evaluation, diet, exercise, grooming, general wellness, and wardrobe.

In Wilkens' second book, *A New You*, two full-page illustrations are devoted to the ideal body as imagined by Wilkens and sketched by illustrator Erica Perl Merkling (Fig. 21). This ideal body is given in both front and side views, showing a young white woman with long, slender legs, small waist, flat stomach, and rounded hips the same width as shoulder and bust.[15] The purpose of the illustration was to give the reader fodder for a self-evaluation, comparing her figure to the ideal.

The first step toward beauty, in Wilkens's opinion, was the personal evaluation, beginning with scrutinizing oneself in the mirror: "coldly, honestly analyze the areas of your own figure that you believe need improvement."[16] Wilkens was not the first to utilize the mirror assessment for a teenage audience—*Calling All Girls* magazine's Margueritte Harmon Bro wrote in 1945, "[G]aze into a full-length mirror while you give yourself an honest analysis. Look at your natural assets and liabilities of form and character, then draw up the *you* of your dreams."[17] Bro used the mirror both literally and metaphorically as she urged her audience to undertake self-improvement of personality, with much less emphasis on changes in the areas of health and appearance; Wilkens's primary emphasis was the reverse.

Anne Hollander argues that it is a misconception that mirrors give us an objective truth about our appearance because we are always posing and mentally constructing a subjective self-portrait; for Wilkens, however, the mirror is the most basic tool for discovering the objective truth about one's looks.[18] In her earlier books for teenagers, Wilkens is explicit in giving instructions on how to go about this process, including taking a full-length "before" photograph, sketching a picture of how one's own figure deviates from the illustrated ideal, and making a list of assets versus liabilities (areas for improvement).[19] In her first spa book for adults, Wilkens takes a tone that assumes her audience is already doing this self-evaluation and addresses the concerns of aging in a culture that admires the youthful beauty she idealized: "(Y)our mirror tells you that your face has fallen a good two inches; a rear view shows dimpling in the fanny; you see patches of flab and cellulite around the hips, tummy, breasts, jowls, and limbs . . . your neck looks as if it belongs on a turkey."[20]

Armed with the results of the personal evaluation, the reader is encouraged to embark on a plan for self-improvement based on Wilkens's other disciplines—or "habits," as she termed them—of beauty, starting with diet. "All men admire a slender beautiful figure," Wilkens instructed her teenage audience, "and there's no one thing that spoils a girl's looks, fun and popularity as much as excess weight."[21] Wilkens had apparently struggled with her weight as a young teenager, and as an adult was committed to the dictum, "A minute in your mouth, a lifetime on your hips."[22]

For Wilkens, a healthy, ideal body started with the building blocks of good nutrition. To this end, she thought of diet in terms of a lifelong process, not just short-term diets for remedying a specific problem (although she did offer these, too). From her very first publication, she spelled out a diet plan that called for fewer calories, was high in proteins, fruit, and vegetables, and reduced starches, processed sugars, and salt.[23] She was a proponent of eating high-iron organ meats and consuming dairy products for bone, hair, and skin health.[24] Wilkens was already an organic foods enthusiast by the 1960s and educated her readers: "Organic foods (those grown without chemicals) are always preferable when you can obtain them, and many stores now offer them."[25] In her concern for eliminating harmful pesticides and other chemicals from one's diet, Wilkens anticipated today's interest in "green" or "eco-friendly" living.

Exercise was another important component of the Wilkens beauty philosophy. While she championed daily outdoor exercise, all her books also include a section on indoor floor exercises.[26] By the 1960s, Wilkens was advocating yoga as a form of exercise that "exalts" rather than "exhausts."[27] Wilkens had likely experienced yoga classes in her visits to health spas, and decades before yoga entered the mainstream she was promoting it as a means of improving physical fitness: "that trim, slim new figure is just ten little yogas away!"[28]

One of the components of beauty to which Wilkens devoted the most space in her books was grooming. "Good grooming" covered a wide variety of activities, from basic bathing to the finishing touch of mascara. For Wilkens, grooming required constant attention: "[G]ood grooming must be a habit, practiced day in and day out, until it becomes second nature . . .

It's the day-in-day-out practice of good grooming habits, you see, that accomplishes results."[29] Wilkens would consistently refer to care of the body as a "habit" to be cultivated, and went so far as to state, "You are the sum total of your grooming habits."[30]

Wilkens scorned the idea that devoting energy to a polished appearance was shallow or frivolous. For her, good grooming was a sign of "personal pride, intelligence and ambition."[31] She rejected the anti-fashion stance of some aspiring intellectuals, crisply noting, "Any girl who slops around in dirty sneakers . . . is broadcasting the fact that she doesn't think much of herself. Maybe she really *is* too busy reading Jean Paul Sartre and dissecting frogs to bother with mundane little things like pushing back her cuticles—but I doubt it."[32] To Wilkens, it was low self-esteem that drove some women to conclude that a grimy appearance and a scholarly pose would help them to be taken more seriously.

Efficient organization was key to good grooming in Wilkens's opinion. In all four of her books, she recommends keeping grooming products and equipment together and well-organized, even if one shared space in a bathroom. Long before the Caboodles organizer fad of the late 1980s, Wilkens suggested keeping supplies arranged together in a hatbox.[33] In her first book for teenagers, Wilkens listed soap, cologne, lotion, bubble bath, and dusting powder as the essential cosmetic products; this core list would continue, though she would later give a more comprehensive list including deodorants and antiperspirants, pumice stones, and products for specific skin conditions.[34]

Good grooming also required an investment of time: "No girl can be really attractive unless she's spotless from head to toe, and it's imperative to set aside a special time every day for acquiring the freshly scrubbed, appetizing, kissable glow that comes from cleanliness."[35] Wilkens believed that at least twenty minutes should be set aside each day for beauty rituals, above and beyond the time required for basic grooming habits such as tooth-brushing, bathing, and facial cleansing.[36] There is something egalitarian in Wilkens's belief that even the realm of American beauty is a meritocracy, in which anyone can be more beautiful through hard work and time invested.

However, as in most other mainstream fashion literature of the twentieth century, the race of her audience is assumed to be white. Wilkens does address the ideal skin tone within the context of sunbathing. "[A] light, golden suntan is both safe and pretty," she asserts, even as she warns, "Overexposure to the sun, however, is dangerous. It can lead to premature aging and wrinkling. . . ."[37] Wilkens's attitude toward sun exposure is fairly cautious, considering the fashionable status of a suntan in the mid-twentieth-century. In the mid-sixties when surfer films deemed the California beach lifestyle the epitome of teenage fun, Wilkens suggested that teenagers cover up under beach umbrellas, large sunhats, and eye-protecting sunglasses and treat their skin with suntan lotion and castor oil around the eye area.[38]

Wilkens's grooming tips for hair included the two-hairbrush method of brushing, which she learned from Elizabeth Arden's spas.[39] Again based on self-evaluation, she recommended specific hairstyles for different face or profile shapes.[40]

Wilkens's books also contain information about makeup. In her books for teenagers, she focuses on the types of cosmetics she believes to be appropriate for teenage girls. For example, Wilkens disapproved of eye shadow for teenage girls except for the most formal occasions: "I don't think eye shadow is at all appropriate for school, street, or even date wear."[41] Wilkens treated makeup as part of a fashionable ensemble, functioning in the same way that accessories such as shoes or a handbag do. Like clothing, makeup was governed by rules of fashion etiquette that dictated what was appropriate for the time of day and type of activity.

While Wilkens's focus in her beauty books was on grooming habits that a woman could carry out herself, and she supports using natural ingredients wherever possible, she does not rule out taking extreme medical steps to achieve the ideal. Even in her advice to teenagers, she anticipates today's blurring of the lines between cosmetic and medical procedures, the most extreme version of modifying the body to conform to the fashionable ideal. Wilkens suggests investigating plastic surgery for "a disfiguring birthmark or a nose that has been your bane for years. . . ."[42]

In general, however, Wilkens asserted that the ideal way to look one's best was through healthiness. In keeping with this, she consistently promoted several practices that can be grouped under the umbrella of general wellness. For example, she believed that getting enough sleep was essential to beauty.[43] Positive thinking and a happy outlook were other wellness factors she stressed.[44] She also believed good posture contributed both to appearance and to health and suggested both physical and mental exercises, such as pretending to be a princess, as a way to improve in this area.[45]

Wilkens also taught that true elegance required maintaining a wardrobe, rather than just accumulating a surfeit of clothes. Wilkens defined a wardrobe as "a collection of clothes you love, in colors that make you happy and pretty, to wear for every occasion."[46]

A 1946 profile of American couturier Mainbocher hailed him as "The 'Cheapest' Dressmaker," because the designer claimed his clothes could continue to be worn for years, and the article reported, "Mainbocher boasts that he spends more of his time discouraging women from buying the wrong things than in selling them the right ones."[47] Wilkens evoked exclusivity and classic taste in the same way through her advice literature, as she cautioned teenagers to buy fewer, better-quality pieces that they could continue to wear. Even as a mass-market dress designer, Wilkens's goal to was achieve more than just a high sales volume; she sought to educate her teenage consumer to purchase wisely.

For Wilkens, a wardrobe was not simply a matter of buying what one loved and hoping it went together: "The secret of elegance is in knowing how to put yourself together so that nothing stands out, but everything looks just right. And this takes planning."[48] A wardrobe required advance strategy, and one of the basic tools for planning was her wardrobe chart. The reverse side of the dust jacket of *Here's Looking at . . . You!* was a blank wardrobe chart for the reader to fill in, and both of her books for teenagers included sample charts.[49] The principles underlying her wardrobe charting were appropriateness and ensemble coordination.

Wilkens believed that wearing the appropriate type of clothing for a particular activity or time of day was just as important for the twentieth-century woman as it had been for her nineteenth-century grandmother.[50] "You can't wear a black chiffon evening dress and spike heels to a football game and feel at ease," Wilkens declared.[51] She divided the twentieth-century teenager's wardrobe needs into four basic categories of day/street, play/sports, date, and late/night.[52] Day/street clothing included dresses, suits, and jumpers in less formal fabrics such as gingham, houndstooth, plaid, and flannel. Play or sports clothing added items such as slacks, shorts, swimsuits, and ski clothes. Date clothes were primarily afternoon-type dresses in more formal fabrics such as taffeta, crepe, and faille. Late/night dresses were in the most formal fabrics and silhouettes (although Wilkens did sometimes design evening clothes that utilized unexpected fibers and fabrics such as woven cottons).[53]

The next step was a thorough closet cleaning and reorganization. The wardrobe chart should be filled in with only the best, most wearable pieces from the reader's current clothes. Determining which pieces fit in with the wardrobe required a ruthless elimination of clothes that were the wrong size or were not flattering, had not been worn in the past year, or did not go with anything else.[54] Clothes that did not fit within these parameters should be given away, and the remaining clothes in the closet organized with dividers into her four categories.[55] Even in Wilkens's later spa books, she allots time for closet organization on day one of her two-day, hour-by-hour home-spa-weekend plan: "2:00 Weed out lingerie and clothes closet."[56] For Wilkens, wardrobe organization was just as essential to overall attractiveness as more conventional beauty treatments.

In discussing closet organization, Wilkens took time to cover clothing maintenance. As part of the American ready-to-wear industry, Wilkens was committed to extending fashion down from the lofty realm of couture to the middle class's buying off-the-rack. Wilkens described this process: "The fashion industry today is attempting to create clothes that fit each individual's personality and figure type, so that all American women can be truly the best-dressed women in the world, even on a modest clothes budget."[57] However, Wilkens knew that no matter how beautiful a garment might be when purchased—whether ready-to-wear or couture—it would eventually look down-at-the-heels without proper care. Democratization of fashion had to address this issue, too.

A fashionable appearance still required the type of detailed clothing maintenance that had traditionally been carried out for people of fashion by household servants. Wilkens wrote from the assumption that the American teenager of the twentieth century would not have domestic staff, and even if she did, it would be helpful for the teenager to learn clothing-care techniques and have a system of making repair notes as soon as a garment is taken off.[58] Wilkens teaches teenagers about clothes-brushing and packing garments in tissue paper for travel—both areas of expertise also covered in *The Butler's Guide to Running the Home and Other Graces*, by English butler Stanley Ager, who worked in service from 1922 to 1975.[59] Wilkens essentially teaches how to act as one's own ladies' maid, making a put-together appearance no longer the sole province of the most privileged.

Finally, with the wardrobe's current contents assessed and well-maintained, it was time to shop for new clothes. Wilkens warned against impulse buying, shopping as entertainment, or purchasing as a pick-me-up.[60] Instead, she advised taking one's wardrobe plan along when shopping, ideally with small swatches of the fabrics of clothes already owned.[61] The goal was to fill in what was needed to create coordinated ensembles. Wilkens encouraged women to buy only what was needed, was well-made, fit with their wardrobe color scheme, and would work for several seasons.[62] "It's all a matter of planning your outfits before you start to shop," Wilkens declared, "If you need a black bag to go with your black shoes, by all means get it the first chance you have . . ."—instead of spending the money on buying eye-catching, unrelated items.[63]

The perfect wardrobe, according to Wilkens, was not a matter of instant gratification. "How long does it take to assemble a perfect wardrobe? Usually about two years for the average girl. If you resolve right now to avoid a single costly mistake, you should soon have more appropriate clothes than you ever imagined."[64] Particularly for a teenager, whose perception of time would have registered two years as unimaginably long, this must have been the most difficult piece of Wilkens's advice to follow.

In the fragmented society of the 2010s, both our bodies and our homes often reflect a disdain of wholeness, with coordination of outfits or rooms disparaged as "matchy-matchy." Nonetheless, Wilkens's principles for organizing and building a wardrobe remain sound advice even in the twenty-first century.

Wilkens's ideal of the body required self-discipline in all areas, from regulating nutritional intake to moderating makeup application to controlling clothing expenditure. The ideal body required effort and showed evidence of the work of fashion from head to toe.

W ell before Emily Wilkens put into writing her ideas concerning the ideal body, she was expressing these thoughts through garment design. Wilkens was in her twenties when she began designing for teens like her younger sisters, Barbara and Janet. She parlayed her relative youth into a big-sister image that—like her dresses themselves—allowed her to mediate between the concerns of her teenage clients and their parents. Wilkens was able to do this, because she was the first prominent designer for teenagers who was not just a creator of, but also a product of, the consumer-goods marketing campaigns that had been targeting adolescent girls since the 1920s.[1] She deeply believed her own messages concerning beauty and appearance. Wilkens's fashion designs were involved in establishing an emerging identity of female, teenage American consumers in the first half of the twentieth century.

A key distinction of Emily Wilkens Young Originals is that in this line Wilkens endeavored to make enduring fashions, rather than just fads, available as a means of self-expression for teenage girls. Magazine editors Gertrude Warburton and Jane Maxwell, writing in 1939, defined a fad as "unrelated to the general fashion trend or in opposition to it, . . . lacking in essential fashion worth, . . . too conspicuous, . . . [and] like a short-lived popular song—catchy but quickly tiring."[2] Despite the

Figure 22. Emily Wilkens's 1953 Patterns of the *Times* design, part of the *New York Times* designer series from Advance patterns.

subjectivity of much of this definition (what exactly constitutes essential fashion worth?), it does help give some perspective on how adults viewed the fads that teenagers created and followed. Teenage fads included writing on garments to personalize them and appropriating items from menswear, such as sweaters, pajama tops or neckties.[3] The do-it-yourself concept that is so associated with the later anti-fashion movement of punk was already well established in teenage girls' culture in the first half of the twentieth century. Kelly Schrum writes that as soon as manufacturers became aware of teen fads, they tried to capitalize on them by mass-producing the items.[4]

While Wilkens did occasionally incorporate fad styles (such as personalization on a dress pattern in the 1950s, Fig. 22), her main goal was to

April 4, 1944.   E. WILKENS.   Des. 137,630
                            DRESS
                     Filed March 7, 1944

Fig. 1.

Fig. 2.

EMILY WILKENS
         INVENTOR

BY   [signature]
              ATTORNEY

Figure 23. Front skirt darts are replaced by smocking on this dress, creating extra ease in the stomach area. Emily Wilkens. Design patent for a butterfly motif dress. Des. 137,630.

give teenagers something closer to adult status, with fashions professionally designed for them. In 1945, *Women's Wear Daily* applauded Neiman Marcus for offering its teenage clientele "some of the new high fashions that teen customers are clamoring for," listing Wilkens's "[d]raped front, built-up skirt in Botany wool flannel" as an example of this high-fashion (rather than basic or simply faddish) clothing.[5] Plate 10 shows an example of a "built-up skirt," which creates a waistline slightly higher than the natural waist.

One of the key ways she designed specifically for teenagers was through fit. Beyond using specific teen sizing for her Young Originals line in 1943, Wilkens aimed to solve teenage "figure flaws" through special design features.[6] For example, Wilkens's clothing for teenagers often included adjustable waistlines.[7] Sometimes this was achieved through smocking or lacing on the bodice (Figs. 17, 19; Plates 1, 7). Sometimes extra ease was created in the stomach area by replacing front darts on a skirt with areas

Aug. 1, 1944.   E. WILKENS   Des.138,430
                                     DRESS
                                Filed July 4, 1944

INVENTOR
Emily Wilkens
BY
ATTORNEY

Figure 24. Again, smock-
ing creates extra ease in
the stomach area. Emily
Wilkens. Design patent
for a rainy-day motif
dress. Des. 138,430.

of smocking, such as in a butterfly motif dress from the Spring/Summer 1944 collection (design patent Des. 137,630), and a rainy-day motif dress from Fall/Winter 1944 (design patent Des. 138,430; see Figs. 23, 24).

Borrowing from childrenswear, on some dresses Wilkens included an attached sash that could also be used to tighten a waistline to varying widths. Some of Wilkens's dresses and skirts for Fall 1945 had separate, adjustable cummerbunds. The Fall/Winter 1945 collection also included a suit and a dress "with side wraps," utilizing the wrap-and-tie flexibility that would later make Diane Von Furstenberg's jersey wrap dresses a success in the 1970s.[8]

Other design details were intended to create the illusion of an hourglass figure. An Empire-style bodice was thought to produce the look of a waistline on a boxy torso (Plates 11, 12).[9] Upper-body details, such as "wings" on shoulders and bodices subtly full to suggest yet-to-develop curves, were balanced by full skirts to minimize waists and hips.[10] Shoulder wings could be made of self-fabric, a contrasting material, or even

Aug. 1, 1944. E. WILKENS Des.138,431

DRESS

Filed July 4, 1944

INVENTOR
EMILY WILKENS

BY

ATTORNEY

Figure 25. Long-sleeved dress with shoulder wings. Emily Wilkens. Design patent for a dress. Des. 138,431.

a trim such as eyelet to visually widen a shoulder often already padded with attached shoulder pads (Plate 1). On some dresses, the shoulder wing itself creates a tiny cap sleeve; on long-sleeve dresses, a wing could be inserted along with the sleeve into the armseye (Fig. 25).

Skirt length was an important design element in negotiating a teenage-appropriate look. In the nineteenth century, a consistent childrenswear theme throughout the decades was that little girls' dresses were cut shorter than those of adult women, even when they otherwise followed the fashionable silhouette.[11] In the 1860s, for example, propriety allowed a girl of four to wear her skirt just below the knee, while a girl of fourteen required a skirt length nearly down to her boot. In a 1947 essay—"Are Clothes Modern?"—based on an exhibition previously held at the Museum of Modern Art, Bernard Rudolfsky referred to this nineteenth-century scheme of girls' skirt-length modesty as "the tantalizing eclipse of the female leg, climaxed by its blackout at puberty."[12]

As the hemlines of adult women rose in the twentieth century, so did

the hemlines of little girls. Daniel Thomas Cook notes that in the twentieth century hemline length continued to be an indicator of a girl's age; he
quotes a 1924 *Babyhood* article that advises an above-knee-length hemline for girls under age ten.[13] Child movie star Shirley Temple tap-danced
and sang through her 1930s films in mini-dresses that revealed a matching panty. Wilkens's childrenswear designs of the early 1940s updated
nineteenth-century childrenswear styles by shortening hemlines above
the knee (Fig. 7).

While today's teenagers may argue for shorter skirt lengths than those
approved by their parents, teenagers of the 1940s wanted longer skirts in
order to appear more grown-up. One young teen wrote into *Calling All
Girls* magazine's "Let's Talk it Over" column to voice her concern that,
"when I wear snowpants and small plain and babyish cotton dresses I am
considered a baby."[14] A twelve-year-old girl who wrote in to this column
was even more specific about her skirt-length problem: "Mother insists I
wear my dresses 4 or 5 inches above my knees. All the girls my age have
dresses at least 1 inch below their knees. I have a name around the school
as 'Jennie short skirts.'"[15] For Wilkens, getting the skirt length right would
be particularly important when designing cotton dresses, which could
sometimes be seen as "babyish" when compared to the bobby-soxer skirt-
and-sweater ensemble. The day dresses from Wilkens's first collections
were shown in just-below-the-knee lengths, which would have pleased the
unfortunate Jennie and young teens like her across the country. Another
teen-friendly feature was a system of "tucks to be let out as the wearer
grew"—again, keeping the correct proportions.[16]

In keeping with general trends in early 1940s fashion, much of the visual interest in Emily Wilkens Young Originals' designs is in the bodice
(Plate 13). In this, she may have been influenced by the work of Elsa Schiaparelli. In the Metropolitan Museum of Art's spring 2012 Costume Institute exhibition *Schiaparelli and Prada: Impossible Conversations*, Harold
Koda and Andrew Bolton observed in a section of the exhibit titled "Waist
Up/Waist Down" that Schiaparelli's design focus was usually on the upper
half of the body.[17] According to many of her fashion world contemporar-
ies, Schiaparelli was the couturiere who best captured the mood of the
era just prior to World War II. "Schiaparelli collections always contained
fashion news in clothes completely suited to modern living in tune with
the times," declared one fashion writer, and an industry executive agreed:

"Schiaparelli . . . the child of her age, made clothes so much in the spirit of the times that they were usually reproduced down to the last crazy button."[18] Schiaparelli's designs had a strong influence on American ready-to-wear and on mainstream fashion generally. Emily Wilkens Young Originals would show the influence of Schiaparelli's motifs of the late 1930s, including butterflies from Schiaparelli's Summer 1937 collection and astrological signs from Schiaparelli's Winter 1938–39 Zodiac collection.[19] Although Wilkens began designing her Emily Wilkens Young Originals line after Schiaparelli's 1941 departure for her wartime sabbatical from the couture, Wilkens's designs show a continuation of Schiaparelli's upper-body focus.[20]

Part of the emphasis on the upper body may also have been practical. The L-85 regulation limited the amount of fabric that could be used for creating decorative hem details. Figure 12 illustrates a dress that might have been manufactured before the regulation went into effect and one that complies with it by limiting trim and eliminating hem interest. Emily had managed to sell her idea for a new line of fashionable, teen-sized clothing despite the yardage restrictions of the L-85 regulation. Also, she had dealt with the problem of wartime fabric shortages by making the deal with Everfast for fabric supply. However, she still had to rise to the challenge of designing something unique that conformed to the L-85 regulation's limits.

The New York Times praised a "young black" dress in Wilkens's first collection "for it was made with a snug bodice and as full a dirndl as the law permits" (Figs. 17, 26).[21] Dirndl skirts, originally based upon peasant styles worn in the Tyrol region of the eastern Alps (in western Austria and northern Italy), had been introduced into American fashion in the 1930s. One writer declared that dirndl skirts "made possible the attractive mother and daughter fashions because both looked so young, fresh and American in the full skirts."[22] Young, fresh, and American were certainly traits that Emily Wilkens Young Originals were designed to convey. Many of the skirts in her early collections were in the dirndl style, as full as possible under the L-85 regulation.

An off-white rayon crepe afternoon dress, probably from 1945 and now in the collection of the Valentine Richmond History Center, also illustrates Wilkens's creativity in meeting the challenge of wartime design (Plate 14). Viewed from the front, the dress seems to have quite a few

Figure 26. The first Emily Wilkens Young Originals collection contained ensembles with coordinating separates or changeable accessories to maximize wardrobe flexibility. Bonwit Teller. "New Designer for the Teens . . . Emily Wilkens." Advertisement. *New York Times*. 16 April 1944.

fabric-consuming bodice details, such as a Peter Pan collar and a peplum at the waistband (Plates 15, 16). But viewed from the back, the dress appears in almost completely pared-down simplicity—the collar and peplum do not extend to the back of the dress (Plate 17). This was one way of saving fabric to keep her designs L-85 compliant—at least for those garments that were actually intended for production, rather than being runway showpieces. See-through trims such as eyelet and crochet were subject to different allowances than opaque fabrics, which perhaps allowed Wilkens freedom to incorporate more of them into her work.

In producing garments she also had to proceed with an awareness of Office of Price Administration (OPA) regulations, which set maximum or "ceiling" prices for new garments. For example, an advertisement for Wilkens's first Young Originals collection lists prices ($13.95 for a pinafore, $5.95 for a blouse, $17.95 for a dress) with small print noting that each of these is the "ceiling price."[23]

The purpose of the OPA's price regulations was to limit the effects of soaring wartime inflation, which had pushed consumer prices up steadily since the fall of 1942.[24] Some articles were assigned a uniform dollars-and-cents retail ceiling price.[25] Other items were subject to more complicated regulations, such as OPA Maximum Price Regulation number 580, dated March 1945, which set ceiling prices for many articles of clothing and household goods based on a system of applying a percentage of mark-up to a net cost.[26] Ceiling prices meant that a designer-manufacturer like Wilkens would have to be careful about keeping costs down, as retailers were limited in the amount of cost increase they could pass on to consumers. Ceiling prices may also have created a barrier to entry for companies in the garment industry—this is another advantage of Wilkens's partnership with an already-established manufacturing business like that of the Chalks. One 1947 source blames a set OPA price ceiling of just $6.95 for teenage dresses for pushing most ready-to-wear manufacturers away from the teenage market.[27] Compared to the $17.95 ceiling price allowed at the time of Wilkens's first collection, the lower price would have certainly created challenges in maintaining quality and profit margin.

One of the signature concepts in Wilkens's early work was the "young black" dress, at a time when black was usually considered too mature a color for young teenagers. The cultural debate over the appropriateness of the color black for teenagers hearkens back to the deb/sub-deb divide and speaks to the issue of how teenagers were classified—were young teens still to be considered children, or were they truly in a transitional phase? A 1945 *Parents'* magazine article voiced the opinion that "most adolescents are still nearer childhood than manhood."[28] Although a scan of childrens-wear—even infants' clothing—in the second decade of the twenty-first century reveals some black garments, the color was not considered appropriate for babies and small children throughout the twentieth century. Writing in 1975 about the various meanings of the color black in Western fashion (including, for example, anti-fashion, dandyism, respectability, and mourning), Anne Hollander concluded, "Presumably, a black layette might still shock."[29]

At the same time, young teenage girls were drawn to the color black precisely because of its implications of sophistication. *Life* magazine reported in December of 1945 that New York debutantes were wearing black dresses for occasions such as tea dances, the theater, and informal dinners, "no matter what the wearer's age."[30] Younger teenagers looked up to, and sought to imitate, the older, junior-miss-size debutante styles. Marketing research conducted in the 1930s by Bamberger's department store, located in Newark, New Jersey, had shown that even then "black evening gowns were the ones that high-school girls buy in spite of parental objections."[31] Presumably, young teenage girls who wanted to purchase black evening gowns would not have been able to find them in the girls' department and would have had to shop in the junior-miss section, dealing with the complications of fit that plagued the fictional Judy Graves. These young women were already exercising agency in selecting a gown in their color of choice; Wilkens recognized this market and designed dresses to fulfill her clients' desires, with age-appropriate fit and styling, such as the "young black" dress.

After an early showing of Emily Wilkens Young Originals, Wilkens's hometown newspaper, the *Hartford Courant*, reported, "Her most startling and dramatic innovation is the use of black touched with color. Needless to say, the girls are mad about black, although this new departure is not generally acceptable to mothers—yet."[32] The *New York Times* had a less conservative take on this same Spring/Summer 1944 collection, deciding that the collection offered "[b]lack that no mother could object to. . . ."[33]

Beryl Williams wrote, "Girls are always eager to get into their first black dress, and they frequently find their mothers reacting with a firm negative when they suggest it. But Wilkens had shown them a way out of this dilemma. She made black dresses with such gay bright accessories that even the most anti-black mother couldn't feel they made her daughter look too old for her age."[34] Fashion and decorative arts writer Elizabeth Burris-Meyer had identified an "[i]ncrease in [the] number of black dresses with bright accessories" in adult women's fashions during the first two years of the war;[35] Wilkens translated this fashion trend for teenage girls.

American custom clothing designer and fashion commentator Elizabeth Hawes viewed the dictum that accessories should match as part of a conspiracy on the part of garment manufacturers to increase sales,[36] but Wilkens disagreed: "You can be perfectly dressed with only two or three of the plainest dresses and suits in your wardrobe if they are properly accessorized."[37] Proper accessorization for Wilkens meant having shoes, gloves, a handbag, and other accessories to match, harmonize with, or contrast with the main garment (Plate 18). Wilkens was a proponent of two different approaches to accessorization: the first was to wear neutral-colored clothes with changeable, colorful accessories, as in the young black dress; the second approach was to buy high-quality, matching sets of neutral-colored accessories that could be worn with many different ensembles.[38] Accessories were key to the Emily Wilkens young black dress and also enabled teenagers to adapt one simple dress for different activities and times of day.

A fashion illustration in a Bonwit Teller advertisement from April 1944 shows "Black Magic," a dress for which Wilkens received design patent Des. 137,566 (Figs. 17, 26). The advertisement describes the dress as a

> "[y]oung black" dress of washable Everfast spun rayon, to wear with change-about accessories, designed by Emily Wilkens, too. Dress, 13.95. Sketched with its sports accessories, plaid gingham jerkin, 4.00 Bag, 3.00 At her knees, caps, belts, flowers, to change the dress for tea-time wear.[39]

The jerkin was a front-lacing vest, shown with the dress in the patent application. This same dress was also profiled in an article, with accompanying photograph, in the *New York Post*, in which journalist Grace de Mun explained that the basic black dress was made of

> an Everfast new linen-finished material called erin. . . . This adorable basic dress was also shown with a jerkin of yellow and black windowpane check laced up the front. Another version showed the dress with

self-material corselet belt laced in front with yellow, mauve and turquoise strings. A third scheme introduced a red-piped black cap and
a gay red and green money pouch slung on a black belt.[40]

Collier's Weekly featured photographs of two young servicemen admir-
ing actress Jeanne Crain wearing this young black dress, worn with the
yellow jerkin, adding the stamp of sex appeal to the ensemble with the
comment: "Lieutenants Duxbury and Erickson approve."[41]

Beryl Williams also writes of this ensemble: "A popular trick for her
black dress with a carefully fitted waist, a full skirt and short sleeves, was a
colorful cotton bodice—low, square-necked and laced up the front. Such
a bodice was not only fun to wear, but it was a special book [*sic*] to the
fatter-this-week-than-last girls."[42] Through the use of a basic dress paired
with changeable, colorful accessories, Wilkens made the color black seem
more useful (perhaps persuading dubious mothers?), and gave her designs flexibility.

Another young black dress, from Fall/Winter 1944, was sleeveless but
had colorful pink and lavender separate sleeves, which could be attached.
Wilkens received design patent Des.138,426 for a similar dress (with a
short-sleeved, rather than sleeveless, underdress, Fig. 27). *Vogue* magazine, in its coverage of "Junior Fashions," compared Wilkens's separate
sleeve design to "'leg sweaters' for her arms."[43] The separate sleeves echo
construction techniques of the Italian Renaissance, when separate sleeves
laced to women's gowns.[44] Wilkens's twentieth-century take on the separate sleeve buttoned at the shoulder, making the buttons both decorative
and functional elements. The dress ($20) and sleeves ($5) were sold sep-
arately.[45]

An extant young black evening dress, c. 1946, has a two-part construction (Plate 11). The bodice is part of the underdress, and a separate,
sheer, pleated skirt is worn over this. The gold-trimmed waistband of the
overskirt, contrasted with the fuller bodice and skirts, works to create the
illusion of a more hourglass-shaped figure (Plate 12). A home-economics
textbook from 1943 illustrates this silhouette as a "modern dress of the
Empire type" and asserts that, "[a] long, clinging dress similar to the Empire type will appear to add height" to the wearer.[46]

The trim of the dress is created from bands of yellow yarn wrapped
in metallic gold foil and is woven in a 2×2 basket weave. A tag inside

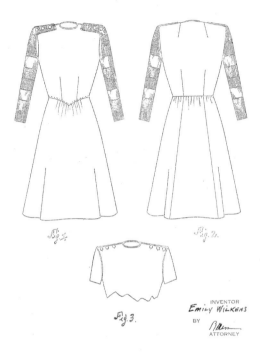

Aug. 1, 1944.   E. WILKENS   Des.138,426

DRESS

Filed May 30, 1944

Figure 27. Emily Wilkens.
Design patent for a dress
with removable sweat-
er-sleeves. Des. 138,426. 1
August 1944.

the dress lists the dress as style number 428, and states that it is a size
nine, which is the smallest size Emily Wilkens made in juniors sizes. The
odd-numbered juniors sizing rather than even-numbered teens sizing
dates the dress most likely to the postwar 1940s, when Wilkens began creating more sophisticated styles geared to a slightly older teenager.

Although much in American women's wartime fashion looked to
menswear and military garb for inspiration, Wilkens's early designs for
Emily Wilkens Young Originals embraced a feminine aesthetic instead:
"Although the fad for shorts, dungarees, and boys' shirts for college girls
was at its peak in 1944" Wilkens was showing dresses with matching parasols (Fig. 28).[47] The parasols added both femininity and historicism to the
overall look of certain ensembles, although one wonders how many teenagers would have actually purchased them. The parasols were not simply
runway props, however—parasols from the 1944 Spring/Summer collection were offered for sale at Bonwit Teller for $6.95.[48]

Figure 28. Dresses with matching parasols. Both dresses now in the collection of Parsons, the New School. Photograph by Eileen Darby. © Eileen Darby Images.

This is not to say that Wilkens did not offer bifurcated garments for her teenage clientele—in fact, quite the opposite. Emily Wilkens Young Originals collections were structured around Wilkens's ideas about appropriateness for the occasion—therefore, the trousers and shorts she designed were created specifically to be part of the "play" segment of a teenager's wardrobe: for the beach, recreation, or at-home wear. Wilkens would not have approved of her shorts designs being worn on the street in Manhattan, or her smock-slacks ensembles worn for studying in the public library rather than at home.[49] Interestingly, in January of 1946, *Vogue* would advocate Emily Wilkens's matador-inspired knickerbocker ensemble from her Spring/Summer 1946 collection as appropriate for resort-wear dining. In the opinion of this author, Wilkens would not have agreed to that usage (Fig. 29, Plate 19).[50]

Shorts were often included as part of coordinated capsule wardrobes advertised to the fashion industry in *Women's Wear Daily* as "country club ensembles" for teens.[51] For example, her first Young Originals collection included the "Week-ender. Little four-piece outfit of Everfast woven stripe chambray to take you straight through from Friday to Monday" (Fig. 26).[52] Wearing the jacket (with sleeves inspired by eighteenth-century

Figure 29. Emily Wilkens did design some trousers, such as these bullfighter pants, or knickerbockers. Photograph by Serge Balkin. Originally published in "Junior Fashions," *Vogue*, 15 January 1946, 100. © *Vogue/Balkin, Condé Nast.*

engageantes) and skirt, the teenager was properly dressed for "tea or a 5 o'clock coke [*sic*] in town."[53] Alternatively, the jacket could be worn with the shorts and then removed to show the white eyelet bra top at the beach (Fig. 11).

Emily Wilkens's inventive separates show continuity with the 1930s American ready-to-wear trend favoring mix-and-match ensembles, which Rebecca Arnold notes were a staple of sportswear lines.[54] An Emily Wilkens Young Originals advertisement from January 1945 shows an ensemble in which a single blouse could take the Emily Wilkens girl from morning to night (Fig. 30). The dark blouse with padded shoulder wings and a plaid bow at the neckline is shown with matching plaid Bermuda shorts for play, with a knee-length plaid dirndl skirt for day or date, and with a floor-length plaid ball skirt for evening.[55] This is probably the ensemble *Women's Wear Daily* described from Neiman Marcus's spring 1945 teen fashions presentation featuring Emily Wilkens Young Originals: "Black was also stressed in the knitted top group, another important fashion for teen-agers, with pink and black plaid taffeta to match both a short and long skirt."[56]

Wilkens's design of separates for the beach also enabled her customers to follow her own cautious attitude toward sun exposure by leaving on outer layers. For example, a 1947 black wool jersey swimsuit came with a blue linen "butcher-boy" jacket, to be worn as a cover-up on the beach.[57]

Wilkens's design hallmarks, from her use of black to her creation of separates, place her squarely within larger trends in American sportswear. In interpreting these looks for the youngest teenagers of the 1940s, she made an innovative contribution to the history of American fashion.

Figure 30. Play, date, or late? This advertisement demonstrates how an Emily Wilkens wardrobe of coordinating pieces, based around a single blouse, allows a teenager to dress appropriately for a range of times and occasions. Emily Wilkens Young Originals, advertisement. Photograph by Toni Frissell. *Harper's Bazaar*, January 1945, 24.

E mily Wilkens had more than enough work to do with designing and managing the successful start of Emily Wilkens Young Originals in 1944, yet she still managed to take time to design costumes for two of the teenage characters of the play *Dear Ruth* on Broadway.[1] In *Theatre Arts* magazine's view, *Dear Ruth* addressed "the comedy angle of what is essentially an un-comic situation, the precocious maturity of the youngest generation under the impact of war."[2]

The years of the Second World War did indeed allow teenage girls to flourish, exerting more agency than ever before. As a society, Americans were ambivalent about this: on one hand proud of these young women as emblematic of the ideals for which they were fighting the war—intellectual freedom, democracy, independence—and at the same time longing to protect teenagers' innocence and keep them from growing up too fast.

Many adults worried about the potential negative side of this increased agency—fearing that teenagers would use this freedom to act out a kind of socially unacceptable despair in response to the pressures and chaotic speed of wartime life. "One way in which we know how damaging can be the effect of all this confusion and disintegration is through increased juvenile delinquency," wrote Alice Barr Grayson in 1944. "Young people are often tempted to adopt the old refrain, 'Eat, drink, and

Figure 31. Lenore Lonergan as Miriam Wilkins in *Dear Ruth*. Richard Tucker/© Billy Rose Theatre Division, the New York Public Library for the Performing Arts.

be merry, for to-morrow we die.'"[3] Delinquency was an extreme reaction to wartime pressures, but the majority of teenage girls did not fall into this pattern. However, even when teens behaved generally responsibly, adults still worried about childhood coming to an end too soon.

Norman Krasna's play *Dear Ruth* captures the spirit of some of these the societal conflicts and offers a satirical view of the precocious teen-ager of the era. It opened December 13, 1944, at Henry Miller's Theatre on Broadway.[4] The overly sophisticated teenage character in question is fifteen-year-old Miriam Wilkins, played in the original Broadway pro-duction by Lenore Lonergan, whom Emily had previously costumed as Fuffy in the stage version of *Junior Miss* (Fig. 31). For months, Miriam has been exchanging letters with Lieutenant Bill Seawright, pretending to be Miriam's grown-up sister Ruth. Bill has fallen in love with the "Ruth" of the letters, and after receiving an early discharge for taking on partic-ularly dangerous missions, has come home to propose. Bill arrives on the doorstep of the Wilkins family just as the real Ruth has become engaged to a different man. When confronted by her parents about the deception, Miriam is maddeningly cool.

Her father exclaims, "This is nothing short of criminal! Who's going to tell him he's been getting love poems, not from a woman, but from an adolescent?"

Miriam replies, "I don't consider myself an adolescent. . . . I'm old beyond my years. I'm quite mature, and I'm equipped to handle this. . . . I'll tell him what I've done. . . . He'll suffer, but in years to come he'll be grateful that I gave him the opportunity to contribute as much as he was capable of in this struggle of our new generation against the old."[5]

Miriam takes an end-justifies-the means approach, viewing her lies as a morale-boosting tool in the service of the war effort, which is just one of her pet causes. She even sees her clothing choices as a form of political activism: the script calls for Miriam to appear in Act I, Scene 1 wearing a beret, which she informs her family is a protest against the State Department's French policy.

The character of Miriam symbolizes much of what adults feared in a generation of teenagers shaped by war: lax moral or ethical standards, romantic precocity, and an overzealous idealism gone wrong. This must have posed a particular challenge for Wilkens's costume designs.

For *Dear Ruth*, Wilkens dressed Lonergan in a simple woven cotton dress with fitted bodice, full skirt, and short sleeves, with contrasting white collar and cuffs (Fig. 31). The basic silhouette of tight bodice and full skirt is similar to many dresses included in the Emily Wilkens Young Originals line.

Whether amused or concerned by the growing autonomy of teenagers portrayed in *Dear Ruth*, audiences would have certainly related. The generational changes Miriam pointed to offered an opportunity for Wilkens to step in and, through her designs, both bridge and exploit what would later be termed a "generation gap."

One of Neiman Marcus's 1945 teen fashion shows offered teenage customers a question-and-answer session with *Seventeen* magazine's fashion editor, Eleanor Hillebrand: "The questions that the teen crowd were most eager to hear concerned hairdos, nail polish, girdles, and the inevitable 'should I dress like my crowd at school,' and 'should mother select my clothes for me?' "[6] Fashion's answer was to dress in what was most becoming to the individual, rather than simply following the advice of peers or parents. Wilkens reached out to these increasingly independent teenagers while reassuring their parents.

For example, in Wilkens's first book, *Here's Looking at . . . You!,* an example of prescriptive literature advising teenage girls on fashion, grooming, health and confidence, she shares the following anecdote: A weekend college house party in Amherst, Massachusetts, in the late 1930s was Wilkens's first opportunity to shop completely for herself. She went to G. Fox & Co., the top department store in her hometown of Hartford and purchased a black date dress, "which fulfilled my dreams of sophistication, and an evening dress, also black, low-cut, and definitely slinky."[7] Wilkens warns her readers that these clothes ended up being too mature-looking compared to the other girls', and left her feeling very embarrassed; she fell back on an old green dance dress that her mother had packed for her, which complimented her red hair, even if it was a bit "babyish." She later credited this weekend as part of her inspiration for designing clothes "at once sophisticated enough to please the girls themselves and simple enough to please their mothers."[8]

The provenance of the 1945 Emily Wilkens Young Originals dress in the collection of the Valentine Richmond History Center offers an example of the way Wilkens's clothes could please both mothers and daughters (Plate 14). Ruby Giragosian (b. 1928) donated the dress to the museum in 1988, noting that her mother had purchased the off-white day dress for her in Richmond. Giragosian had worn the dress for her "best dress," to church and other formal day occasions when she was seventeen and eighteen. While Giragosian was a couple of years older than the brand's target audience, as a student of and then graduate of Richmond's John Marshall High School, she was part of the high school demographic Wilkens intended to reach.

Wilkens sought to create the right style balance in her designs, older-looking than girls' clothes, but not too grown-up.[9] Journalist Virginia Pope wrote, "She felt her object could best be achieved in persuading the junior, and then the teen-ager, to get out of the sloppy sweater and skirt outfit and to put on a trim and pretty dress."[10] The *New York Times* also reported, "Now the teen-age girl has a designer of her very own, one who understands her problems and gives her clothes that are 'hers'—and not ideas handed down from grown-ups, or elevated from the 'horrible' little-girl sphere."[11] Labor historian Susan Porter Benson has suggested that this idea of relating to the customer's problems—also included in theories of successful selling in retail stores' salesclerk training—accorded well with accepted notions of "femininity" such as showing empathy and meeting others' needs.[12] Both working woman Wilkens and her teenage clients were thereby framed in the media as exerting agency in a way that was nonthreatening to the social order.

It is within the context of this tension between the new freedoms that teenage girls were enjoying and concern about pushing them out of childhood too fast that Wilkens's work with her Young Originals label achieved national recognition.

As discussed in the introduction, one of the most significant awards Wilkens won was third prize of the 1944 American Fashion Critics Awards, sponsored by Coty (known as the Coty Awards). The Coty Awards had been founded two years earlier, the brainchild of Wilkens's own publicist, Eleanor Lambert, with the goal of "draw[ing] attention to the originality, scope and power of American fashion and bring[ing] it to equal prominence with European fashion."[13] Wilkens was given a $500 cash prize and a silver plaque at the Coty Awards show on February 13, 1945, at the Waldorf-Astoria Hotel in New York City.[14] At the time, Wilkens was the youngest designer, and the only designer of teen clothes, to have received a Coty Award.[15] Along with the first-prize-winner Adrian and second-prize-winner Tina Leser, Wilkens showcased her latest designs in a runway fashion show and participated in a ceremony with New York City Mayor Fiorello H. La Guardia presenting the prizes.[16] The fashion show was staged by visual merchandiser Lester Gaba, who would be a long-term friend of Wilkens. Gaba's design for the show included ballet-inspired blue lighting and an S-curved, ramp-style runway that started backstage and extended into the audience seating area.[17] Wilkens wrote of the 1945 Coty Awards show:

> The fashion show that followed the luncheon was staged with all the fanfare of a major first night on Broadway, with elaborate backgrounds, spotlights, and props carrying out the teen-age theme of my collection. A lithe young girl in a brief gingham bathing suit skipped across the stage bearing aloft a hot dog three feet long. Next came a

Figure 32. "Heart-thrill" day dress of "Victorian gray cotton" from the 1945 Coty Awards fashion show. Photograph by Eileen Darby. © Eileen Darby Images, Inc.

cute junior in a bright cotton play dress, sipping a giant strawberry soda. She was followed by a model in a date dress, carrying a phonograph record the size of a wagon wheel.[18]

A photograph in *Life* magazine shows a dress "of Victorian gray cotton with a white rolled collar"; the model, with light-brown or blonde hair, appears to be holding the giant strawberry soda that Wilkens mentions (Fig. 32)[19]. Each of the fashion-show props mentioned references other aspects of teenage consumer culture—foodways, music—that were already so ingrained in the public imagination that they could act as a visual shorthand for the concept of "teenager." The message of Emily Wilkens's portion of the fashion show was clear: the teenage girl was a consumer—of food, record albums, and now teen-specific fashion.

It has been well established that the years of the Second World War, when American clients were cut off from the Paris couture, brought American designers into the spotlight and gave them an opportunity to showcase their creative ability.[20] The designs of the three winners of the 1944 Coty Awards represent several sources of inspiration adopted by American fashion designers after the cutoff. The Hollywood glamour and

Figure 33. Evening dress, same as sketch number 615 (Plate 3) from the Brooklyn Museum collection, shown at Bonwit Teller fashion show. Originally published in "New Young Styles," *Life*, 18 March 1946, 88. Photograph by Herbert Gehr/Time and Life Pictures/Getty Images.

Americana of Adrian and the exoticism and influence of non-European cultures in the sportswear of Tina Leser have been well-documented.[21] In her Spring/Summer collection the following year, Wilkens would show fellow-prize-winner Leser's influence in an Emily Wilkens Young Originals halter-top evening gown with bare midriff (Fig. 33, Plate 3).

Wilkens's work is grounded both in the American sportswear tradition and in another source to which American designers turned for inspiration—American history, discovered through museum research. According to *Life* magazine, Wilkens received the Coty Award "for her Victorian-inspired teen-age clothes"; she represents both the trend of historicism and museum research for design inspiration and the forward-looking trend of youth-inspired fashion.[22]

For the Coty Awards fashion presentation, Emily Wilkens showed a group of clothes from her Spring/Summer 1945 collection titled "Keepsake Fashions," which was inspired by "the pretty ruffles of 1860–1900 [combined] with the practical play themes of 1945."[23] *Life* also describes the day dresses she featured: "Eyelet embroidery like that used on underwear 50 years ago is used as trimming on both these dresses, one pink, one blue."[24] An 1880s corset cover from the collection of the Costume In-

Figure 34. Dress with eyelet trim from the Spring/Summer 1945 collection (left), shown with nineteenth-century undergarments that inspired it. Photograph by Eileen Darby. © Eileen Darby Images, Inc.

stitute (C.I.42.15.1), was one source of inspiration that Wilkens acknowledged for "Keepsake Fashions."[25] In a photograph from the spring of 1945, a model wearing one of Wilkens's eyelet-trimmed spring dresses is shown next to a model wearing the nineteenth-century corset cover (Fig. 34). The eyelet trim was a motif used in many pieces, including striped day dresses, in that collection.[26]

1940s commentators compared Wilkens's work to the nineteenth-century illustrations of Kate Greenaway, noting Wilkens's pinafore motif, which had already been present in her earlier childrenswear designs.[27] Rebecca A. Perry has written about Kate Greenaway's historicizing influence on nineteenth-century girls' clothing; in the concluding chapter of her master's thesis, Perry mentions Wilkens as an example of "the lasting influence of Greenaway's aesthetic." Perry asserts that Wilkens "was inspired by Greenaway's illustrations," thereby placing Wilkens as a twentieth-century successor to Greenaway's embrace of the past and the pastoral as a space for childhood innocence and as an antidote to the evils of modern, urban life.[28]

Figure 35. Wilkens studying garments at the Museum of Costume Art, now the Costume. Institute. Author's collection.

I have not uncovered any evidence that Wilkens was directly inspired by Kate Greenaway. The "Greenaway" label as used by writers of the 1940s seems to have been just another way of describing the garments' historical feel. Wilkens's fashion designs were inspired neither by Greenaway's sketches nor by her reforming ideals, but rather by extant late-nineteenth-century garments, both children's and adults', representing the mainstream of fashion. Journalists of Wilkens's day, as well as the late fashion curator Richard Martin, have noted that museum research of historic garments was integral to Wilkens's design process; she particularly liked the Museum of Costume Art, now the Costume Institute (Fig. 35).[29] Beryl Williams wrote of Wilkens, "Emily used the charming clothes of the 1870's as the basis for her first collection. . . . She is, she says, an inveterate user of the museums of costume art and the art collections, and she doesn't see how anybody can design without knowing them well."[30]

Martin compared Wilkens's nineteenth-century-inspired designs to costumes from the musical *Oklahoma*, and I think this reference is an apt one.[31] Beneath the joyous songs, sense of community, and nostalgia of *Oklahoma* there is a dark undercurrent of economic transition, loneliness, and sexual frustration, which are belied by the modest frills of the costumes. Similarly, Wilkens's designs for teenagers employ historicism in ways even more complicated than in her own childrenswear, where the purpose might be quaint cuteness and a straightforward protection of innocence. Wilkens's teenage clothes carry out a balancing act, using historicism to invoke innocence but at the same time acknowledging a budding sexuality and a middle ground between the responsibilities of the child and the adult.

Interestingly, there is a literal connection to *Oklahoma!* through an article in *Vogue* magazine from February 1945, "The American Ballet Girl Look," which featured *Oklahoma!*'s ballet choreographer, Agnes De Mille, in a photo spread surrounded by dancers clad in Emily Wilkens play clothes.[32] A more important link between Wilkens's historicism and theater costume is that, just as theater-costume designers often use historic research as a departure point rather than a detailed dictate, Wilkens's designs do not obsessively copy the past. Rather, they interpret it, and often the correlation to the historic garment might be missed unless her design was seen side-by-side with its inspiration.

Pairing each new Wilkens design with the historic garment it references was exactly the technique used in a series of photographs by Eileen Darby taken in the spring of 1945. A pink-and-white striped two-piece evening dress in Everfast cotton was photographed next to a nineteenth-century child's dress with similar center-back bustle bow and hem flounces (Fig. 36). Martin, writing in *American Ingenuity* in 1999 just after exhibiting the extant Wilkens evening dress (now in the collection of Parsons, the New School), notes that Lambert's original press release for this dress emphasized its historicism: "[I]t is clear from Lambert's assertion of the 'bustle-type bow' that the paradigm of American history . . . constitutes an integral part of the 'selling' and promotion of this dress. Some lingering sense of a Golden Age America continued to hold powerful sway. . . ."[33]

A similar photograph was taken of a yellow day dress from the same

Plate 1. This day dress includes many of the quintessential Emily Wilkens Young Originals features, including shoulder "wings," expandable smocked bodice, sash tied at the back, and a dirndl skirt. Emily Wilkens. Fashion sketch number 607, Spring/ Summer 1946. Ink, pencil, and watercolor on paper. Brooklyn Museum Libraries. Special Collections. The Fashion and Costume Sketch Collection. Courtesy of Hugh Wilkens Levey and Jane Wilkens Michael.

Plate 2. This daytime suit was appropriate for wear in the city and for occasions such as luncheons or church attendance. Emily Wilkens. Fashion sketch number 614, Spring/Summer 1946. Ink, pencil, and watercolor on paper. Brooklyn Museum Libraries. Special Collections. The Fashion and Costume Sketch Collection. Courtesy of Hugh Wilkens Levey and Jane Wilkens Michael.

Plate 3. An evening gown in a fabric inspired by nineteenth-century ribbon shows the influence of Wilkens's fellow Coty Award honoree, Tina Leser, in its halter-top bodice. The back bustle recalls fashions of the 1870s and 1880s, while the bare midriff invokes modern daring. Emily Wilkens. Fashion sketch number 615, Spring/Summer 1946. Ink, pencil, and watercolor on paper. Brooklyn Museum Libraries. Special Collections. The Fashion and Costume Sketch Collection. Courtesy of Hugh Wilkens Levey and Jane Wilkens Michael.

Plate 4. Detail of 1940s Emily Wilkens Young Originals label. Private collection. Image © Lolly Koon.

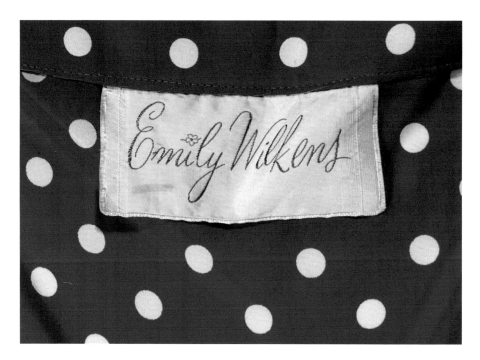

Plate 5. Detail of 1950s Emily Wilkens label. Private collection. Image © Lolly Koon.

PORTRAIT OF A YOUNG GIRL IN A POSTWAR FABRIC

"Sunmere" by Everfast* is the first of the miracle fabrics. Woven by Ponemah Mills of
1.0 denier rayon, it is silken in texture and as easy to wash and iron as all
fabrics by Everfast*. Emily Wilkens has styled it for teen-agers in a group of dresses
in copen, turquoise, pink or maize, to be found exclusively at **Bonwit Teller** in New York. About $23.

Ponemah

SPUN AND WOVEN

* Reg. U. S. Pat.

THRU A RING — THE SIGN OF A FINE FABRIC

Plate 6. This dress of Everfast Sunmere rayon features historicizing eyelet trim threaded
with black ribbon, inspired by Wilkens's museum research. Ponemah Mills advertisement. "Portrait of a young girl in a postwar fabric." *Harper's Bazaar*, March 1945, 133.

Spring 1946

Plate 7. Illustration of a dress with smocked bodice, similar to that for which Wilkens received design patent Des. 144,473. Emily Wilkens. Unnumbered fashion sketch. Spring/Summer 1946. Ink, pencil, and watercolor on paper. Brooklyn Museum Libraries. Special Collections. The Fashion and Costume Sketch Collection. Courtesy of Hugh Wilkens Levey and Jane Wilkens Michael.

f

Plate 8. Newly "discovered" model Tee Matthews represents the Emily Wilkens ideal of beauty in an Emily Wilkens Young Originals Spring/Summer 1944 cotton dress. Photograph by Toni Frissell. *Vogue*, 14 May 1944, 100. © *Frissell/Vogue, Condé Nast.*

Plate 9. Rust red–and-black striped taffeta afternoon suit, missing one of its original buttons. Emily Wilkens Young Originals, afternoon suit, rayon, Fall 1945. Private collection. Photograph by the author.

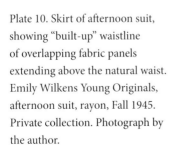

Plate 10. Skirt of afternoon suit, showing "built-up" waistline of overlapping fabric panels extending above the natural waist. Emily Wilkens Young Originals, afternoon suit, rayon, Fall 1945. Private collection. Photograph by the author.

Plate 11. Two-piece "young black" evening dress with chiffon overskirt. Emily Wilkens Young Originals, evening dress, rayon, c. 1946. Private collection. Image © Lolly Koon.

Plate 12. Detail of "young black" evening dress bodice and waistband of separate skirt. Emily Wilkens Young Originals, evening dress, rayon, c. 1946. Private collection. Image © Lolly Koon.

Plate 13. Dress with "Quaker collar." Emily Wilkens. Fashion sketch number 606, Spring/Summer 1946. Ink, pencil, and watercolor on paper. Brooklyn Museum Libraries. Special Collections. The Fashion and Costume Sketch Collection. Courtesy of Hugh Wilkens Levey and Jane Wilkens Michael.

Plate 14. Front view of Ruby Gira-gosian's "best dress." Emily Wilkens Young Originals, day dress, rayon, 1945. Reproduced by permission of Valentine Richmond History Center.

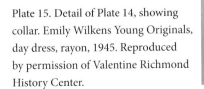

Plate 15. Detail of Plate 14, showing collar. Emily Wilkens Young Originals, day dress, rayon, 1945. Reproduced by permission of Valentine Richmond History Center.

Plate 16. Detail of Plate 14, showing peplum. Emily Wilkens Young Originals, day dress, rayon, 1945. Reproduced by permission of Valentine Richmond History Center.

Plate 17. Reverse view of the dress pictured in Plate 14 shows that fabric was saved by not continuing the peplum and collar to the back of the dress. Emily Wilkens Young Originals, day dress, rayon, 1945. Reproduced by permission of Valentine Richmond History Center.

Plate 18. Navy suit with barrel-shape skirt and matching hat, bag, and shoes. Emily Wilkens. Fashion sketch number 602. Spring/Summer 1946. Ink, pencil, and watercolor on paper. Brooklyn Museum Libraries. Special Collections. The Fashion and Costume Sketch Collection. Courtesy of Hugh Wilkens Levey and Jane Wilkens Michael.

Plate 19. Knickerbocker or bullfighter pant ensemble. The young woman Wilkens sketched resembles the designer herself. Emily Wilkens. Fashion sketch number 613. Spring/Summer 1946. Ink, pencil, and watercolor on paper. Brooklyn Museum Libraries. Special Collections. The Fashion and Costume Sketch Collection. Courtesy of Hugh Wilkens Levey and Jane Wilkens Michael.

Plate 20. Navy cocktail dress with bertha collar. Emily Wilkens for Reich Goldfarb, c. 1951. Private collection. Image © Lolly Koon.

Plate 21. Navy crepe evening dress with sequin trim. Emily Wilkens Young Originals, evening dress, probably rayon, c. 1946. Private collection. Image © Lolly Koon.

Plate 22. Navy crepe evening dress with sequin trim, reverse. Emily Wilkens Young Originals, evening dress, probably rayon, c. 1946. Private collection. Image © Lolly Koon.

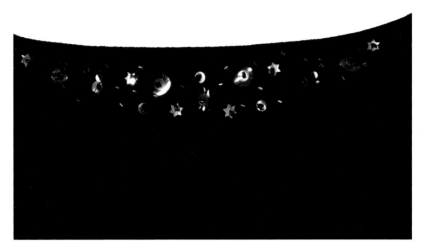

Plate 23. Detail of navy crepe evening dress with sequin trim. Emily Wilkens Young Originals, evening dress, probably rayon, c. 1946. Private collection. Image © Lolly Koon.

Plate 24. Pal Fried. Portrait of Emily Wilkens (Mrs. Irving Levey) with her children, Hugh and Jane. Oil on canvas. Courtesy of Hugh Wilkens Levey and Jane Wilkens Michael.

Plate 25. Strapless evening dress in red with white polka dots. Emily Wilkens for Reich Goldfarb, c. 1951. Private collection. Image © Lolly Koon.

Plate 26. Crinoline in hem of strapless evening dress in red with white polka dots. Emily Wilkens for Reich Gold-farb, c. 1951. Private collection. Image © Lolly Koon.

Plate 27. Strapless evening dress in alternating sheer and opaque black stripes. Emily Wilkens for Reich Goldfarb, c. 1951. Private collection. Image © Lolly Koon.

Plate 28. Emily Wilkens for Bonwit Teller. Fitted coat. Fashion sketch number 106 with swatches. Fall 1953. Courtesy of Hugh Wilkens Levey and Jane Wilkens Michael.

Plate 29. Emily Wilkens for Bonwit Teller. Suit with paisley blouse and tie. Fashion sketch number 103 with swatches. Fall 1953. Courtesy of Hugh Wilkens Levey and Jane Wilkens Michael.

Plate 30. Emily Wilkens for Bonwit Teller. Coat, skirt, and blouse. Fashion sketch number 317 with swatches. Fall 1953. Courtesy of Hugh Wilkens Levey and Jane Wilkens Michael.

Plate 31. Emily Wilkens for Bonwit Teller. Suit with cravat and coat lining of paisley. Fashion sketch number 318 with swatches. Fall 1953. Courtesy of Hugh Wilkens Levey and Jane Wilkens Michael.

Plate 32. Emily Wilkens for Bonwit Teller. Red day coat. Fall 1953. Private collection. Image © Lolly Koon.

Plate 33. Emily Wilkens for Bonwit Teller. Red day coat. Fashion sketch number 104. Fall 1953. Courtesy of Hugh Wilkens Levey and Jane Wilkens Michael.

Plate 34. Emily Wilkens for Bonwit Teller. Red day coat, label. Fall 1953. Photograph by the author. Private collection.

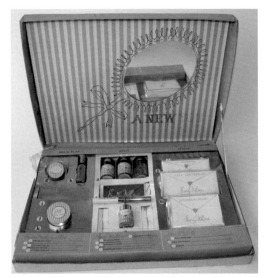

Plate 35. Emily Wilkens *A New You* home beauty kit prototype. Photograph by the author. Collection of Hugh Wilkens Levey and Jane Wilkens Michael.

Plate 36. Emily Wilkens *A New You* home beauty kit, exterior view. Photograph by the author. Collection of Hugh Wilkens Levey and Jane Wilkens Michael.

Plate 37. Emily Wilkens *A New You* home beauty kit prototype, makeup chart. Photograph by the author. Collection of Hugh Wilkens Levey and Jane Wilkens Michael.

Figure 36. Evening dress of pink-and-white striped cotton with bustle bow in back (right), shown with the nineteenth-century child's dress that inspired Wilkens's design. Photograph by Eileen Darby. © Eileen Darby Images, Inc.

Spring/Summer 1945 collection (that extant dress is also now in the collection of Parsons, the New School) (Fig. 37). This dress offers an example of Wilkens's combining multiple historic references in a single garment. A newspaper clipping from February 1945 suggests that the draped sleeves and "low-cut" back neckline on this yellow Sunmere rayon dress were drawn from a daguerreotype.[34] Martin writes that the idea for the smocking on the shoulders may have stemmed from a rust-colored cotton dress from the Costume Institute (C.I.41.2.1), from around 1888.[35]

The newspaper clipping specifies that the ribbon on the neckline and bodice is black velvet and shows that the technique of threading it through eyelet was used on other garments in Wilkens's summer 1945 collection, including a "breakfast coat" and halter-neck "overalls" (which appears to be a one-piece garment we would term a "jumpsuit" today).[36] The black-ribbon-through-eyelet motif can also be seen in the pink Sunmere rayon dress advertised by Ponemah Mills (Plate 6).

Figure 37. Yellow Sunmere rayon dress with black velvet ribbon threaded through eyelet trim (left), shown with nineteenth-century child's dress that inspired the cut of the bodice. Photograph by Eileen Darby. © Eileen Darby Images, Inc.

Black ribbon has a historic association with mourning in children's clothing, as black ribbon and embroidery were considered proper for babies and children in mourning in the nineteenth century.[37] However, Martin asserts that black ribbon threaded through eyelet was a Wilkens trim detail originally inspired by a c. 1900 plaid child's dress from the Costume Institute.[38] Given that the dress Wilkens had studied was plaid, it is likely that even in the original the black ribbon was a purely aesthetic choice rather than intended to indicate a state of loss. It is interesting to see how meanings of the color black changed over time, given the importance of that color in Wilkens's work. Martin notes that Wilkens used this black ribbon trim on the extant yellow dress, and that this "became an abiding motif for her work."[39]

While Wilkens acknowledged her museum-object inspiration for the threaded ribbon motif, this device also may have resonated for personal reasons—Wilkens may have been unconsciously mining her childhood.

Figure 38. "Dream dress" from the 1945 Coty Awards fashion show, inspired by an 1820 miniature. Photograph by Eileen Darby. © Eileen Darby Images, Inc.

A baby photo shows her in a knit romper with satin ribbon threaded through the eyelet neckline (Fig. 1).

The previously mentioned *Life* article also shows an evening dress: "An 1820 miniature inspired this dress made of white ruffled organdy. Fabric limitations make this a design for post-war" (Fig. 38).[40] In looking to an art-historical past, rather than to a Parisian present, Wilkens at the same time anticipates the long, full-skirted postwar silhouette associated with Dior. Journalist Virginia Pope noted that each Wilkens collection included "a dream dress of floating tulle or net with a big bow sash at the back in baby pink or blue—these to please doting mammas."[41] According to the original museum catalogue card of an extant version of this dress, it was the "dream dress" of Emily's Spring/Summer 1945 show. It is now in the collection of Parsons, the New School. Just as contemporary couture runway shows sometimes present models that will never be realized commercially but are considered good advertising for the more commercially viable ready-to-wear, here Wilkens is using the award presentation fashion show as a promotional vehicle to promote her regular line.

Due to wartime restrictions, much of what is historicizing in Emily Wilkens Young Originals dresses of the World War II years is in the trimming. The Valentine Richmond History Center's off-white dress is a perfect example of this. It is essentially a simple dress that hangs from the narrow shoulders; viewed from the back it looks modern (Plate 17). The cleverness of Wilkens's design lies in her ability to evoke the past for her audience by layering a veneer of historicizing details (like a peplum and a series of twenty-four covered buttons with self-fabric loops down the bodice front) over that modern dress (Plate 16).

Wilkens continued to look to the past for inspiration in her work. Even in the 1950s, when much of the fashionable silhouette was in and of itself historicizing, Wilkens continued to use specific historically inspired motifs. For example, a 1951 ballerina-length juniors evening dress was made in a printed white lawn with a small purple figure from Fuller Fabrics, inspired by an 1850s print.[42] An extant navy cocktail dress, probably dating from 1951, has a bertha-style neckline reminiscent of women's dresses of the 1840s (Plate 20).

Another source of inspiration for designers in the United States during World War II was to look to the Americas. American Indian motifs, as well as design elements from Central and South America, were part of this trend. One commentator wrote, "The . . . slim wrap-around skirts of the South American Indians suggests a fashion possibility for modern adaptation to brilliantly colored cotton clothes, since the clothes of these peoples fit into the trend for brilliant color and 'Good Neighbor' policy of the early forties."[43] The United States' "Good Neighbor" policy and related design movement was not limited to fashion; Walt Disney and an entourage of artists, including graphic designer Mary Blair, embarked on a goodwill tour through South America in search of inspiration.[44] In 1941, Dorothy Shaver of Lord & Taylor wrote in the introduction to Edouard Halouze's *Costumes of South America*, "In this country now face to face with its own designing ability we find the colorful source material of our neighbors in the South American republics rich in costumes of ineffable beauty."[45] Halouze's book of color plates showcases motifs from a variety of folk and indigenous costumes of South America and was intended to both record vanishing styles of dress and offer new thoughts to American clothing designers.

Figure 39. Beach ensemble in a Seminole-inspired pattern. The model is carrying the matching skirt. Originally published in *Life*, 18 March 1946, 88. Photograph by Herbert Gehr/Time and Life Pictures/Getty Images.

While the Americas trend was a less common source of ideas for Wilkens, she did contribute to this area of American design. For four days in October 1945, the *New York Times* staged its "Fashions of the *Times*" runway presentation, showcasing American designers. "Designers of suits, dresses, sportswear fabrics and millinery were invited to go to the city's museums and find ideas to develop," reported Pope in the *New York Times*. "The result was fantastic."[46] Wilkens's contribution was a three-piece "Seminole playsuit" beach ensemble, based on an Indian woman's dress that Wilkens discovered at the Costume Institute. She had the blue and pink colors copied on a Mallinson jersey.[47] The "Fashions of the *Times*" press coverage would be seen as a boon for both the Mallinson company and Wilkens. She then used this well-publicized print in her Spring/Summer 1946 collection, which included the beach ensemble as well as a halter-top evening dress with a solid-color bodice and the Seminole-inspired print on the skirt (Fig. 39).[48]

The Seminole-print garments form an interesting bridge, showing Wilkens's typical museum-researched design method applied even when creating a look not based on the history of Western fashion.[49] Wilkens would later return to the Americas trend with a colorful postwar beach ensemble utilizing an Everfast cotton piqué fabric in an oversized pansy print with a South American, Carmen-Miranda-style exuberance.[50]

Wilkens was not the only person designing for the newly recognized teen market, but she would be the designer to garner the most critical attention. In addition, Emily Wilkens Young Originals advertisements fed into coverage in feature articles, and vice versa. An ad Wilkens ran in *Women's Wear Daily* after her first showing at Bonwit Teller made the most of the editorial coverage she had received, touting, "Press acclaims Emily Wilkens in Bonwit Teller Premiere."[51] An article in *Women's Wear Daily* two weeks later suggested,

> The interest which New York retailers are suddenly showing in teen
> fashions and the advertising space being devoted to them . . . is wor-
> thy of notice. Many people in the trade have offered the opinion that
> with the appearance of Emily Wilkens teen designs and their exciting
> presentation by Bonwit Teller in New York, and one important store
> in key cities across the country, the entire teen dress market is being
> spurred to greater originality in design.[52]

New York manufacturing businesses such as Sporteens, Inc. and Teen Frocks, Inc. had been supplying dresses for the teen market since the early 1940s, but they had not captured the spirit of fashion as Emily Wilkens Young Originals did.[53] Pope reported that Wilkens's designs were part of a current trend: "Now the teen-age girl is stepping into the forefront where fashion is concerned. . . . Young women, not so very far removed from their teens themselves, are designing for her. They understand her prob-lems: they know she is an individual with specialized tastes. From bathing suits to party dresses she now has styles of her own."[54] In Pope's article, Wilkens's designs are shown alongside those of Frances (at Franklin Si-mon), as well as clothes from unnamed designers at Altman, Saks, and Abraham & Straus.[55]

A prominent competitor in the teenage market was Teen-Timer (sometimes spelled TeenTimer) Originals. While the Emily Wilkens Young Originals business was focused on a named designer and the con-cept of high-fashion exclusivity, Teen-Timer's was a more mass-market undertaking and only occasionally credited its designers, such as Grace

Norman.[56] Manufacturer Jules Rubinstein started his Teen-Timers, Inc., business in 1943, the same year that the Emily Wilkens Young Originals partnership was formed, and within four years Teen-Timers would go on to open ninety-eight franchised stores in which their garments were sold.[57] Teen-Timers responded to the initial Emily Wilkens Young Originals coverage in spring 1944 with a nearly full-page advertisement in *Women's Wear Daily* encouraging teenage department buyers to "[m]ake your store solid with the teen crowd! by featuring the big Teentimer Original "Design-and-Name-It" contest." The contest encouraged its teen customers to design and name an outfit in the hopes of winning a prize of US war bonds and promised store buyers their teen department would "positively sizzle with activity" when they featured this contest, which Teen-Timers would back up with national advertising including newspaper, radio, and movie slots.[58] The Teen-Timers business would, in fact, outlast Emily Wilkens Young Originals, with Teen-Timers continuing in the teen clothing business into the 1950s.[59]

So why were Emily Wilkens Young Originals such a standout? Part of the answer must lie in her business model and the fact that as a named designer she was easier to recognize. Beyond this, her work itself was compelling at this specific moment in American history. Her wartime designs got more publicity than they might otherwise have received had American designers been competing with those in Paris for media attention. Furthermore, during the war teenage fashions represented a much-needed bit of good news—wholesome teen fashions acted as a counterbalance not only to growing concerns about juvenile delinquency, but also to the gruesome and relentless reports of war. Emily Wilkens Young Originals were at once modern and historicizing. I would argue that it is this combination of female agency and American tradition that both the fashion industry and the American public found so uniquely reassuring in 1944–1945, leading to Wilkens's many awards and accolades.[60] Emily Wilkens Young Originals evoked the simplicity of the American pioneer daughter, the innocence of the Victorian girl, and at the same time, all that was best about the modern American teenager: freedom used responsibly.

Wilkens herself was also newsworthy in a positive way. Sources give the narrative of Wilkens primarily as a typical American success story, showing her as an example of how individual effort and talent can pay off, even for a young woman. Unspoken in the media of the 1940s, but clearly present from the vantage point of our century, is the contrast between persecution and genocide of Jews in Axis-controlled sections of Europe and the hope offered by the glamorous success of a young Jewish woman in the United States.

Wilkens went on to win several other awards for her designs. On August 31, 1945, Wilkens flew to Dallas, Texas, where she would receive a Neiman Marcus award for distinguished service a few days later.[61] While there, Wilkens visited the home of Stanley Marcus, and was very impressed by the efficiency of the wardrobes of his two daughters, teenage Jerry and slightly younger Wendy. She would later cite the Marcus girls as exemplars of taste and organization:

> [N]either girl possessed a single unnecessary item. Their clothes were carefully arranged and well cared for—no garments strewn over beds and chairs . . . And they were very proud of the clothes they had, took care of them, and kept them in order. Later, I commented to their mother on this unusual state of affairs, and she told me that she and their father had been careful never to let the girls have more clothes than they needed, even though they had a whole store at their disposal.[62]

On December 27 of this same year, Wilkens was recognized again, one of nine young women to receive a *Mademoiselle* magazine award for "signal achievement" for 1945. The awards were presented by Betsey Talbot Blackwell, editor-in-chief of the magazine. The award itself included a $25 war bond in a green leather pocketbook. Other winners included Dr. Leona Woods Marshall, a physicist, and the poet Gwendolyn Brooks.[63]

In October of 1946 she was further honored, this time by *Fashion Trades* magazine with a Ten Best Designers award (also known as the Golden Thimble).[64] New York Governor Thomas Dewey presented the awards.[65] Wilkens was one of ten winners representing various aspects of the fashion industry, including Lilly Daché, Gilbert Adrian, Nettie Rosenstein, and Claire McCardell. Daché and Wilkens are pictured together in the *Times* article, placing Wilkens's fashion significance among the well-established names of American fashion.[66]

From the perspective of good design and critical acclaim, Emily

Wilkens's fashions for teenagers were a clear success. But more than just good design is involved in making a label a success in terms of sales. Marketing and distribution are also key, and Wilkens was well aware that she would need to use all available resources to take her brand message across the nation.

The marketing efforts for Emily Wilkens Young Originals reflect developments in fashion marketing to teenagers in general. Emily Wilkens was especially timely in choosing to start designing for teenagers in the early 1940s, just as teenagers were exerting new levels of agency in the marketplace. As Jessie Stuart wrote in a 1951 brochure for an audience of retail salespeople:

> The youth movement, which has made itself felt in so many phases of American life since World War I, brought into the apparel industry two specialized fields, the junior miss and the teen-ager . . . As clothes began to be designed for these groups, fashion magazines emphasizing their interest appeared on the newsstands: *Mademoiselle* for the college girl and young matron; *Charm* and *Glamour* for the business and career girl; and *Seventeen* for those still in their teens.[1]

Seventeen began publication in September 1944, the year after Wilkens launched her teen-sized Young Originals business.[2] *Seventeen* was the first magazine to focus on the teen demographic (as opposed to the slightly-older-geared magazines listed by Jessie Stuart, or magazines like *Calling All Girls*, which spoke to a slightly younger crowd). Sociologist Kelley Massoni credits *Sev-*

enteen's first editor-in-chief, Helen Valentine, with the original idea for a service magazine written specifically for teenage girls.[3] Valentine originally limited *Seventeen*'s editorial fashion coverage to teen-sized clothing, barring the more mature juniors sizes.[4]

Seventeen's appeals to advertisers claimed that prior to their publication "[d]ecent dress designers" ignored teenagers—an exaggeration that minimized Wilkens's achievements.[5] However, the new *Seventeen* was a boon to the teen-size clothing industry and would be followed by a standalone version of *Junior Bazaar* in November 1945.[6] Interest in the teenage market was high enough that *Junior Bazaar*'s first independent issue weighed in at 275 pages, which *Life* magazine stated was a record for a popular magazine's inaugural issue.[7] The staff of *Junior Bazaar* had an average age of twenty-one and included photographer Richard Avedon, who was twenty-two.[8] In the same month that *Junior Bazaar* first appeared on newsstands, Wilkens turned to the advertising firm Gravenson Company to craft her ads for trade and consumer magazines.[9]

Marketing aimed at teenagers was not without criticism. However, at least some of the individuals who were involved in marketing to teenage girls genuinely believed they were helping them. Massoni states that *Seventeen*'s early promotions director, Estelle Ellis, thought that the growth of the teen consumer "would lead to the increased status of teens . . . as they became more valuable to the economy, they would become more valued citizens."[10] Massoni quotes Ellis as saying, "these young people were entitled to be respected by the retailers of this country, by the advertising agencies of this country, by the manufacturers of products!"[11] American teenage girls of the 1940s were exercising agency as consumers, making their own decisions about the clothes they wore—and, of course, Wilkens was poised to cater to this growing demand.

Bernice Chambers wrote in 1947:

> The adolescent daughter, often left to her own devices during World War II while her mother was absorbed in war work, emerged as a personality with definite tastes, and with a way of life and buying habits all her own. Stores that formerly sold teen-age clothes in the girl's department are now catering to this new person with displays and merchandise that meet her approval in a separate department.[12]

Stuart also observed, "The importance of the teen-age girl and the college girl in the American social scene is much greater than in Europe where, even now, the young girl tends to stay more in the background than her American counterpart."[13] Chambers similarly drew this distinction between teenage American girls and those across the Atlantic: "In many European countries, unmarried girls do not assume authority or select their own clothes. In America, teen-age girls buy a surprisingly large amount of fashion merchandise and make their own selections."[14] Kelly Schrum argues that this had been the case for quite a few years before the 1940s, with the numbers of teenage girls shopping without their mothers growing steadily in the 1920s and 1930s.[15] Schrum's argument is supported by Anne Rittenhouse's 1924 observation in her book *The Well-Dressed Woman*: "Girls have become the arbiters of what they wish to wear. Mothers are advisors or purse holders and if other duties have kept them out of the swift-flowing current of fashion, they are not always consulted as to the choice of a wardrobe."[16]

In the 1940s, increasing numbers of girls were continuing their education through high school. Most public high schools offered classes in home economics, with textbooks that assumed that high school girls were already involved with shopping for clothing, at least for themselves. One textbook notes in its introduction, "To the High-School Girl": "Emphasis has been placed on the present-day problems of the consumer because, as a consumer, you have many demands on your time and money."[17] To help teenage girls in their current and future roles as consumers of clothing, home-economics texts offered advice on wardrobe planning and budgeting.[18] For a nation at war, wise shopping took on a new urgency, and girls were admonished, "One of the most important contributions you can make to the war effort is to conserve the clothes you have, to select new clothes wisely, to learn to make many of your clothes, and to make over for your own use or that of younger members of the family garments that would ordinarily be discarded."[19]

In the first half of the twentieth century, department stores set the standard for the American shopping experience. These large stores were the major source for the teenage consumer. Even in 1949, the National Retail Dry Goods Association's manual for buyers admonished, "We must not forget that the customer still looks to her favorite store for leadership in what is new and correct in fashion. . . ."[20] Department stores and large specialty stores of the mid-twentieth century offered many age-specific departments "for the infant, the pre-school child, the school child, the teen-ager, the debutante or college girl, the young woman, and the older woman."[21] However, in the early 1940s, the concept of a teenage department, separate from the little girls' department, was still a relatively new one. Even OPA regulations grouped teenage sizes with children's and toddlers' size ranges, and *Women's Wear Daily*'s coverage of the teen market was in the "Children's Wear" section.[22]

But wise merchants were beginning to recognize that the female teenage shopper would be more impressed by being treated as a young woman rather than as a child, and that this distinction could result in increased sales. Physical separation of the teen section from the childrenswear section on the selling floor was crucial in marketing to teenagers. For example, Neiman Marcus in Dallas saw a dramatic increase in sales when it moved its teen clothing section away from infants and childrenswear and gave the teen department its own entrance.[23] Teen departments also often grouped their clothing offerings with other teen-targeted items such as special cosmetics and accessories, anticipating the boutique concept that would gain popularity in the 1960s and avoiding the issue of interselling between departments.[24]

Another factor in the shopping experience and agency of teenage girls in the 1940s was the interaction between the teenage customer and the salesclerk. A 1944 article, "Selling Teenage Coats and Suits" informed the saleswoman that the teenage customer "may have definite clothes ideas, but her own unguided selections are not always the best. With understanding and tact, you can help every young customer to be her most attractive self."[25] The article also noted that especially in the case of younger teens, the girl's mother might also be in the background. A successful sale would have to take into consideration the desires of both mother and daughter, with the saleswoman sometimes acting as mediator in conflicts between the two. Articles like this served to reinforce the salesclerk's idea of herself as an arbiter of fashion and taste, though clearly at the expense of the agency of the teenage girl.[26]

The beginning of the change to self-service schemes in stores carrying ready-to-wear helped to shift the dynamic of the sale slightly, giving more power to teenage consumers. Prior to World War II, saleswomen had controlled access to department-store merchandise.[27] A customer would be shown perhaps three garments at a time by a saleswoman who retrieved the garments from a case and then accompanied the customer to the dressing room.[28] However, with labor shortages during the war, many large stores were forced to try new self-service methods of selling ready-to-wear, taking their cue from the grocery store context, in which chain stores like Piggly Wiggly had implemented self-service shopping decades earlier.[29] In order to compensate for the lack of salespeople, ready-to-wear retailers began using open displays of garments through which customers could wander and make their selections unassisted.[30] As much as the new plans meant reduced customer service and a decrease in the direct power of saleswomen, this may have suited teenage customers perfectly—especially those who shopped without their mothers—empowering them to make their selections with less adult assistance.

In 1944, the fashion-industry magazine *Women's Reporter* ran an article about retail's response to the new teenage customer. The article's author, Cora Carlyle, asserted, "By far the most dramatic job of cashing in on this revolutionary new consumer market has been Bonwit Teller, on Upper Fifth Avenue."[31]

Bonwit Teller was technically a large specialty store, rather than a department store.[32] According to the National Retail Dry Goods Association,

> Many stores of large size are completely departmentalized, as in the case of the large city clothing stores, yet are not called department stores. A more generally accepted definition would be one that describes a department store as having usually a large sales volume, handling a wide variety of merchandise, including dry goods, women's wear, men's wear and home furnishings, arranged departmentally, with a buyer or manager in charge of each department, and operated as though it were an independent store unit.[33]

Clothing consultant Margaretta Byers wrote in 1941, "the difference is simply that a specialty shop sells primarily apparel while a department store also sells yard goods, home furnishings, and so on. The department store is usually bigger. And it's generally not quite so 'high style' as the specialty shop."[34]

Bonwit Teller was noteworthy among specialty stores in having a female president, Hortense Odlum, who had been brought in by her husband's investment group in 1934 to revamp the store. Odlum was not afraid to go against conventional retailing wisdom in making changes that she believed would please customers, and it is probably this spirit of openness to new ideas that put Bonwit Teller at the forefront of the new teenage market in the early 1940s.[35]

In late 1943, as Wilkens was developing her Emily Wilkens Young Originals line, Bonwit Teller already had a Teen Age Department buyer, Charlotte Christianson.[36] In April of 1944, Christianson was reported as being Bonwit's buyer for childrenswear as well as teenage clothing, but by November of that year she was reported to be a dedicated buyer for teenage clothes, perhaps showing the success of her new Teen Age Department.[37] Christianson was not by any means the only buyer of teenage clothes in the industry. In March 1944, even regional stores such as C.C. Anderson in Boise, Idaho, were opening teen departments, and the teenage clothing market was expanding so rapidly that buyers of teen clothing considered starting their own association.[38] In the nineteenth century, most store buyers had been given free rein and functioned as autonomous heads of their own departments; while their mid-twentieth-century counterparts were less likely to enjoy complete autonomy, they were still powerful figures in the store hierarchy.[39]

Christianson would have been a key contact for Wilkens. Wilkens met with Christianson, who advised and encouraged her, sharing her experience on the retail side of the fashion industry.[40] *Women's Wear Daily*'s coverage of the first Emily Wilkens Young Originals fashion show suggests that the premiere of Wilkens's line was closely tied to the launch of Bonwit Teller's "new Tween Teen Girls Shop."[41]

Women's Wear Daily's article about the first Emily Wilkens Young Originals fashion show also included a quote from Bonwit Teller's vice president and sales promotion manager Sara Pennoyer: "'these are not wasp-waisted junior fashions; they are designed expressly for the teenage girl, taking into consideration the needs and tastes of that age and figure.'"[42] Pennoyer had worked in advertising copywriting, buying, and fashion reporting and had once been promotion director at *Harper's Bazaar*.[43] As an example of the "small world" of the New York fashion industry and Wilkens's growing connections within it, Pennoyer was also the former boss of Wilkens's publicist, Eleanor Lambert; Lambert had found her first job in New York working for Pennoyer at the Amos Parrish advertising agency.[44] In short, Pennoyer understood the need for the right publicity to connect customers with fashion merchandise.

Under Pennoyer's leadership, Bonwit Teller featured dresses from the Emily Wilkens Young Originals Spring 1944 collection in special window displays.[45] Bonwit Teller's teen-specific marketing also included meetings for teenagers in addition to fashion shows. In a tactic anticipating early-twenty-first-century reality television and social media, teenagers were encouraged to vote for their favorite styles, but also to critique and give feedback on the store's offerings.[46]

The care put into the design and marketing of Emily Wilkens Young Originals seems to have paid off in sales. *Women's Wear Daily* reported, "According to Mrs. Christianson . . . the [Emily Wilkens Young Originals] clothes have met with outstanding success ever since they arrived in the department a few weeks ago."[47] The success of Emily Wilkens Young Originals and the teenage department of Bonwit Teller seem to have been interlinked and mutually beneficial.

Wilkens made the most of marketing opportunities provided by retailers, which were also developing formal public relations departments around this time.[48] The relatively new field of public relations, as applied in the department-store context, led to fashion shows, teen departments, and teen clubs, which were used to draw young consumers and build store loyalty in the years before they shopped for trousseaus. Stores from Rich's in Atlanta to The Fair in Chicago developed in-store teen clubs in the 1940s, and by 1947 The Fair's teenage club membership would number more than eight thousand.[49] Drawing on the model the college boards used to promote back-to-school clothing purchases by using college students' peers as salespeople and advisors, stores implemented high school boards, "with the dual purpose of sales promotion and securing information about the special requirements in clothes and accessories for the high school age."[50]

The G. Fox & Co. department store in Wilkens's hometown of Hartford, Connecticut, hosted fashion shows of Emily Wilkens Young Originals clothing and was one of the stores to feature a dedicated Emily Wilkens section.[51] In her book *Here's Looking at . . . You!* Wilkens recounts one of her fashion shows at G. Fox & Co. in the mid-1940s. Wilkens describes how she would stand at a microphone and provide commentary on the various ensembles as they came out.[52] She gives this example of the typical patter that might accompany one of her designs down the runway: "'We call this one Tea for Two. . . . It's the kind of dress that will turn a mere movie date into a big evening. The trick is in the simple lines and lack of ornament. You can wear a string of pearls with it and not look overdressed.'"[53]

Fashion shows like those at G. Fox or Bonwit Teller gave Wilkens an opportunity to interact with her young clients, showing them the ideal look complete with grooming and accessories. Shows also gave her a chance to explain what made her clothes special from a design point of view ("simple lines and lack of ornament"), and to contextualize the clothes that might otherwise be first encountered just hanging on the rack ("the kind of dress that will turn a mere movie date into a big evening"). Helping teenagers know when and how to wear her clothes was just as important as the garments themselves, particularly in the mid-twentieth century, when observing rules of clothing etiquette for various venues and times of day was crucial to projecting respectability.

Fashion shows also gave Wilkens a chance to answer teenagers' questions. At one 1946 fashion show at Bonwit Teller, teenagers posed two questions to Wilkens—one was how soon they could get the new fashions, and the second was whether a girl needed to be thin in order to wear Emily Wilkens Young Originals. Eugenia Sheppard's newspaper coverage reported Wilkens's answer, which was in keeping with Wilkens's beliefs regarding beauty habits: "Suits and dresses already have gone into action on the store's seventh floor, Miss Wilkens said, and a girl who can't wear them, with their carefully manipulated stripes and slimmed-down waists, had better take to a hard and fast diet."[54]

Sometimes Wilkens did more than just comment on her fashion parade, giving a didactic talk to her teenage audience that anticipated her later work as a motivational speaker. For example, as part of her presentation to hundreds of Dallas teenagers at a fashion show and boxed-lunch event celebrating her Neiman Marcus award in 1945, Wilkens also showed sketches (later given away as prizes) and draped on a form. She used these visual aids to illustrate how some of her designs emerged from the qualities of the fabric itself and others were based on research. "In explaining the use of source material she had a museum costume modeled, and then showed a partially finished spring dress in which were incorporated many features of the costume. She then asked the girls how they would like to have it trimmed."[55]

Wilkens also participated in the new medium of television as a promotional tool for her line. As early as March 11, 1944, the Philadelphia Gimbels department store presented a television review:

> On Sunday night, through the newest medium of sight and sound, we give you a glimpse of what happened in Philadelphia this past week. Scenes from the brilliant Assembly Fashion Show. Interviews with four famous designers—Sally Victor, Emily Wilkens, Rose Barrack and Madame Tsang . . . The program has been specially arranged for our many guests from the New York area who, because of war-time limitations, were unable to travel to Philadelphia this year.[56]

Television was a media outlet Wilkens would continue to use later in her career.

By 1947, Wilkens had made a name for herself in the world of fashion and was considered enough of a celebrity designer for Milliken Woolens to use her photograph in an advertisement in *Seventeen* showcasing "Pert! Emily Wilkens's Bow-Tie Dress!" made of "Milliken's sheer wool and worsted," and featuring debutante model Pat Geoghegan (Fig. 16).[57] The Milliken Woolens ad was part of a series; Milliken also ran ads in *Life* showing Vera Maxwell's picture alongside her "Poet-Suit" of Milliken wool and a photograph of Rose Barrack sketching beside her "Torso Dress."[58] In using Wilkens's photograph to sell the product, this ad places her, like Sally Milgrim and Valentina, within an American fashion tradition of promotion using the designer's photograph in magazine spreads and advertisements.[59]

Emily Wilkens Young Originals did not spring to life in a marketing vacuum. Wilkens's success was fostered by the increasing agency of teenage girls themselves, as well as a range of promotional efforts that reached out to teenage consumers, selling both Wilkens's designs and her persona as a youthful American designer. Wilkens's fashion cachet in turn gave luster to the channels that promoted her, from the new teenage departments in stores to fabric companies.

W orld War II came to a close with the surrender of Japan in August 1945. Although wartime regulation of the American fashion industry did not immediately disappear, people were ready for a change of mood. Many fashion changes were on the horizon. It was time to recharge, reassess, and move forward.

Recharging for Emily Wilkens came with what she termed her "first fairy-tale visit" to cosmetics mogul Elizabeth Arden's spa, Maine Chance, in 1946.[1] This would mark the beginning of a lifelong pattern of spa-going, from which Wilkens would glean tips, soak up the atmosphere, and be revitalized. Maine Chance, open since 1934 and located on a plot of Maine farmland, was the first real luxury spa in the United States, dedicated to both health and beauty.[2] At Maine Chance, spa-goers had beauty treatments, participated in exercise classes, and then dressed for dinner, which was an elegant but diet-conscious affair.[3] Wilkens delighted in the different settings of china each night, the monogrammed sheets, the pampering of breakfast in bed.[4] Wilkens visited Maine Chance many times, and Arden gave her a wicker bed-top vanity tray bedecked in Arden pink as a present. Wilkens would later reminisce about her first Maine Chance stay: "The war had been over for a year, and we wanted to forget it had happened. The days of

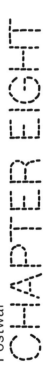

rationing were past, and we celebrated their passing with indulgences. Maine Chance was, for me, a supreme self-indulgence."[5]

This same spirit of indulgence brought changes in the world of fashionable dress. By autumn of 1946, US fashion restrictions implemented during the war were being slowly loosened to avoid dramatic changes in silhouette. Changes were made allowing for the reintroduction of pleats, facings, shirrings, and pockets. Wilkens greeted this development with approval, saying that now designers could "have some fun, . . . design the way we want."[6] However, American designers were still far from being able to introduce dramatic changes. While Norman Norell and other designers were eager to lengthen skirts, this was made impossible both by continuing fabric shortages and reports announcing "[r]estrictions on length and sweep of skirts were being retained . . . to prevent a breakdown of the Office of Price Administration's pricing structure."[7] Wilkens did expand into higher price points after the war, with day and date dresses in the $20–$30 range and an evening dress of blue rayon chiffon with black ribbon selling for $60 in December 1946, in contrast to the $17.95 ceiling price allowed for dresses from her first collection.[8]

Rebecca Arnold writes, "Once America had entered the war in 1941, fashion magazines repeatedly used a range of signifiers to construct a more complex visual landscape, which showed everything from red, white and blue colour combinations to explicit references to the war effort."[9] Wilkens continued to use this color scheme even after peace was declared. One extant Emily Wilkens Young Originals long-sleeved evening dress combines a dark navy blue crepe fabric with "star-spangled" cuffs and back neckline (Plates 21, 22). These areas are trimmed with stacked blue and silver sequins, silver six-pointed-star-shaped spangles, red bugle beads and red flower spangles (Plate 23). This dress still contains the paper tag stating that it is style number 471 and juniors size fifteen—the largest size in which Emily Wilkens Young Originals were available in the late 1940s.[10] The box-pleated waistline of this dress is similar to that of a brown strapless evening dress from Wilkens's Fall/Winter 1946 collection, which was featured in *Vogue*.[11]

In February 1947, the Paris couture house of Christian Dior presented Dior's first collection—titled "Corolle" but more popularly known by Carmel Snow's designation, "The New Look"—and ushered in a fresh, abundant and feminine silhouette.[12] Fashion journalist Ernestine Carter would recall:

> The first Dior collection was unforgettable: the model girls arrogantly swinging their vast skirts (one had 80 yards of fabric), the soft shoulders, the tight bodices, the wasp-waists, the tiny hats bound on by veils under the chin. To us in our sharp-shouldered (a legacy from Schiaparelli), skimpy fabric-rationed suits, this new softness and roundness was positively voluptuous. All round the salon you could see the English tugging at their skirts trying to inch them over their knees.[13]

From this moment into the 1950s, the luxury of the French couture would challenge the ready-to-wear sportswear aesthetic of most American designers and vie for American customers.

Yet the reality across much of Europe was still one of deprivation and fabric shortages, epitomized in Wilkens's February 1947 designs for CARE (Cooperative for American Remittances to Europe). For ten dollars, Americans could send packages containing virgin wool Army-surplus blankets and food to war-devastated areas of Europe. CARE also asked several American designers, including Wilkens, Claire McCardell, Madame Eta, and milliner Lilly Daché, to create sample garments using the olive-drab Army-surplus blankets, with the idea that the patterns for these garments would eventually be included in the CARE packages (and also certainly to create publicity for the charity efforts). Wilkens's contribution was a simple juniors-size suit, which could be made from a single blanket.[14]

Wilkens's own collection, shown February 6, 1947, at Bonwit Teller, marked changes in her thinking, which *New York Times* fashion journalist Virginia Pope described:

> For some time she has been talking about doing a more sophisticated type of dress; that at last she has realized her ambition was evident. . . . Now this able young designer will create for the young lady with the Emily Wilkens type of figure until she is ready for her senior prom. Miss Wilkens . . . called attention to the somewhat lengthened skirts, which have come down one to one and a half inches.[15]

Bonwit Teller would sell the Spring/Summer 1947 Emily Wilkens collection both in its Teen Shop and in a special Emily Wilkens Young Clothes section on its seventh floor, perhaps reflecting both teen- and juniors-size offerings.[16] Wilkens acknowledged that for this collection she was inspired in part by menswear, and the resulting clothes have a much more tailored look.[17] This is a departure from her earlier super-feminine designs and—apart from the lengthening skirts—seems oddly out of step with the postwar fashion direction, which Dior would come to epitomize.

It is almost a cliché that in the postwar period traditional gender roles were reinforced both in fashion and in American society as the Paris couture stole the spotlight from American female ready-to-wear designers and returning servicemen filled jobs held by women during the war. However, the drama of work/life demands on married women in the postwar period is precisely what seems to play out in Wilkens's career and personal life.

On December 21, 1947, Wilkens married New York Supreme Court Justice Irving Lawrence Levey, who was almost twenty years her senior (Figs. 40, 41).[18] According to her children, Wilkens met their father while vacationing in Cuba.[19]

By 1946, air travel was making it possible for American tourists to again plan getaways to the Caribbean, even while most passenger ships had not yet been reconverted to peacetime use. Cuba was an easily accessible ninety minutes by plane from Miami.[20] The spirit of postwar indulgence predominated in the pre-Castro Cuba of the late 1940s, making it a popular destination of yacht clubs and nightlife, which has been compared to a tropical Las Vegas.[21] In December of 1946, *Life* magazine reported that Havana was

> the heart of the West Indies. . . . Cuba today is almost like prewar Paris in its gaiety. Visitors splurge on duty-free French perfumes and alligator bags and shoes. . . . They bask in the sun or swim along miles of golden beaches. At night they gamble at the swanky but rather dull Casino Nacionale or find real excitement in the native cabarets and outdoor cafes where the rumba bands rattle on until dawn.[22]

Wilkens met Levey when "they were both guests of others in Havana and it was at the Havana Yacht Club which was a very 'social' place to be

Figure 40. Portrait of New York State Su-
preme Court Justice Irving Lawrence Levey.
Detail. Oil on canvas. Courtesy of Hugh
Wilkens Levey and Jane Wilkens Michael.

at the time."[23] Judge Levey was apparently quite an eligible bachelor and
had not been married before. Three hundred people attended his bachelor
dinner.[24]

The newlyweds also honeymooned in Cuba, but Wilkens's connections
to the world of fashion and beauty followed her even there. The intrepid
Estée Lauder later recalled that Wilkens "'probably didn't expect me to
show up in Havana on her honeymoon so I could test my creams on her
skin in the sun.'"[25] But Lauder did exactly that.

Once the honeymoon was over, like many working women of the era,
Emily Wilkens now had to face the very real challenge of how to combine
marriage and a career. As late as 1939, over half the state governments of
the United States had made attempts to outlaw the employment of married women in an effort to spread wages and a subsistence income to as
many families as possible.[26] Culturally, in many circles there continued to
be an expectation that women would not work for wages outside the home
after they were married.[27] With her marriage, Emily Wilkens sacrificed
her Emily Wilkens Young Originals business.

Wilkens withdrew from active design work for a time, except for occasional projects such as a Cinderella dress for the "Fashions of the *Times*"
fashion show.[28] However, in 1948, Wilkens published her first book of
prescriptive literature, *Here's Looking at . . . You!*, written for teenage girls
about topics including beauty, fashion, diet, organization, and etiquette.

Figure 41. Emily Wilkens with her father, Morris Wilkens, on the day of her marriage to Irving Levey, December 21, 1947. Courtesy of Hugh Wilkens Levey and Jane Wilkens Michael.

She dedicated this book to her husband somewhat cryptically, using just the initials I. L. L.[29] A 1949 press-release biography stated that Wilkens was in the process of writing a novel to be published by Putnam, which had also published her first book.[30] The novel, however, does not seem to have materialized. In 1949 Mr. and Mrs. Levey had their first child, a son named Hugh Wilkens Levey; a daughter, Jane Wilkens Levey, would follow (Plate 24).[31]

According to Hugh, Wilkens would sometimes say in retrospect that she had stopped working when her son was born because he was sick. However, both of Wilkens's children agree that childcare was not her strong point. Each child had a personal nanny, with relatively little hands-on time from Wilkens. Hugh recounts one time that his nanny outfitted him in his snowsuit before she left for her time off, leaving Hugh in the care of his mother. When the nanny returned several hours later, Hugh was still in the snowsuit.[32]

Hugh speculates that the business closure perhaps had more to do

Figure 42. Emily Wilkens's Fall 1950 Patterns of the *Times* design, part of *The New York Times* designer series from Advance patterns.

with Wilkens's husband not wanting her working so closely with other men (such as her business partners, the Chalks). Wilkens's daughter Jane ascribes her mother's "retirement" to more general pressure for married women of her social position not to work.[33]

It is also important to remember the volatility of the garment manufacturing business. While Emily Wilkens Young Originals had only been in existence for about four years, in the 1940s it was axiomatic that the average life of a garment manufacturing business was just eight years.[34] Many American garment manufacturers went out of business each year, and Emily Wilkens Young Originals was just one of the 691 clothing firms that closed their doors in 1947, outnumbering the 445 new companies that opened.[35] Within the American ready-to-wear industry, this was usually thought of as "turnover" rather than "mortality," "for though many firms go out of business, most of the same faces reappear year after year, in a new firm or reorganization."[36]

Whatever the reasons for dissolving the Emily Wilkens Young Originals partnership, after just a couple of years away from designing, Wilkens was poised to try a career comeback.[37] Professionally, she would continue to be known as "*Miss* Emily Wilkens" even after her marriage—this was a common formulation in the fashion industry in the years prior to the alternative title "Ms.," used both for designers who had made a name for themselves prior to marriage and for department-store saleswomen regardless of their marital status.[38] In August 1950, Wilkens debuted an Advance home sewing pattern as part of the *New York Times* Patterns of the *Times* Designer Series(Fig. 42).

In an era when many women found it more affordable to sew at home rather than buy ready-made clothing, Wilkens's creation of a home sewing pattern was a way to reach a wider clientele that might not normally be able to afford her ready-to-wear designs. Budget-conscious mothers and even teenage girls sewed at home, with additional sewing instruction available for teenagers through high school home-economics classes as well as places like their local sewing machine stores. A Singer Sewing Center brochure of 1948 advertises Singer's "Teen-Age Sewing Course in 8 lessons" for teenage girls twelve to seventeen and urges parents, "Rates are so low for Teen-Agers that many parents have told us that the saving on their daughter's class-made dress almost paid for the entire course!"[39] Wilkens's creation of home sewing patterns was a marketing effort akin to high/low pairings of designer names producing capsule collections for discount retailers such as H&M and Target in the twenty-first century. Through this pattern mothers, or the teenage girls themselves, could capture the Emily Wilkens look for less.

The separates ensemble featured in the 1950 Advance home sewing pattern, while containing a weskit as in some of her earlier designs, aimed at an older demographic than her Emily Wilkens Young Originals line of the 1940s. Now she was designing for the older teenage girl going back to college.[40] This is indicative of the direction Wilkens's designs would take in the 1950s, as she began to create more sophisticated, juniors-size clothing.[41] For example, Emily Wilkens garments would be featured as honeymoon play clothes for the trousseau of a young bride.[42]

Wilkens explained in 1950, "Because I have a junior-size figure myself, and intend never to lose my young ideas about clothes I am well aware of the need for specifically 'junior' designed clothes for young women of all ages."[43] As a newspaper guest columnist, Wilkens explained what the junior figure entailed: a shorter waist and shorter waist-to-hem measurement than misses sizes as well as a less-full bust.[44] As in her previous work with teen sizes, one of Wilkens's main preoccupations was with proper fit, which, along with figure-flattering styles, would make her clients look their best.

Although at first glance it seems odd for Wilkens to move away from the teen-sized clothing for which she had been acclaimed in the forties, this choice may have been in keeping with broader trends within the industry. There seems to have been a continual aspiration upward to juniors-size clothing. For example, *Seventeen* magazine had originally limited its editorial coverage to teen-sized clothing; Kelley Massoni notes that under pressure from the magazine's owner, Walter Annenberg, *Seventeen*'s editorial pages began to include juniors sizes in 1948.[45] In later years, Wilkens became so associated with the juniors market in public consciousness that one history of the ready-to-wear industry written in 1975 would omit her ground-breaking work in the teen market altogether, listing her only as a designer of junior-miss clothing.[46]

One major difference between Wilkens's work of the 1940s and her foray back into the garment industry in the early 1950s was that instead of being a partner in her own company, she now worked for others, although she remained a named designer. In 1950 and 1951, she was associated with the wholesalers Reich-Goldfarb; her clothes were still sold at Bonwit Teller, and she also did some exclusive collections for the specialty store.[47]

Reich-Goldfarb advertised itself as a corporation with offices at 530 Seventh Avenue, a building in the garment district between West Thirty-Eighth and Thirty-Ninth Streets.[48] The Art Deco–style 530 Seventh Avenue building had been designed by Ely Jacques Kahn specifically to meet the needs of the fashion industry. Completed in 1930, the building still serves as headquarters for a variety of fashion-industry tenants.[49] Reich-Goldfarb had been in the business of manufacturing women's dresses at this location since at least the beginning of the 1940s.[50] The company would also continue in the dress business after the departure of Wilkens.[51]

Wilkens brought her own vision and ideas to bear in her early 1950s designs, even as she paid more attention to the undergarments required to attain the hourglass fifties figure. Wilkens sold colorful cotton-net petticoats in red, blue, pink, and white.[52] One of Wilkens's twists on the full-skirted silhouette of the early 1950s was the "petti-sheath"—a garment of cotton flannel with a boned strapless bodice, which could be worn as a petticoat or as a dress.[53] She also designed a petticoat with a built-in waist cincher, in an effort to simplify the crucial 1950s underpinnings.[54]

The problem with Emily Wilkens's juniors-size designs from the fifties is that while she is certainly keeping pace with fashion, her garments are in general not as distinctive as her Emily Wilkens Young Originals of 1944–1946. Many dresses are not distinguishable at first glance from her competition in the juniors market, such as Anne Fogarty of Margot (who promoted what she termed the "paper doll" silhouette).[55] A 1956 home-economics textbook lists both Fogarty and Wilkens in its group of seven "well-known American designers since 1917."[56]

A few years earlier, a 1949 home-economics textbook had credited Wilkens's career with "stimulat[ing] the interest of teen-age girls in attractive clothes and also in choosing careers in fashion designing."[57] Tellingly, Wilkens was seen as encouraging agency in her teenage clientele, even just a few years after debuting her line. The 1956 textbook echoes these thoughts and adds Fogarty's name, drawing a comparison between the target clientele of the two designers: "Emily Wilkins [sic] and Anne Fogarty created a greater interest in high-school girls for attractive clothes and increased their desire for careers in fashion designing."[58] The success Wilkens and Fogarty achieved at relatively young ages was an encouragement to teenage girls that they, too, might find rewarding careers within the fashion industry.

Despite competing demands of family and work, Wilkens also found time for philanthropic activities. She was on the committee for the International Silk Association USA's "World of Silk" fashion show benefitting the United Nations International Children's Emergency Fund in September 1950.[59] In December of that year, she donated fashion dolls dressed by her to be auctioned off to benefit the (New York) Handicapped Children's Home Service.[60]

Part of Wilkens's 1950s marketing strategy seems to have been the "beauty queen" tie-in. For example, advertising from Spring 1951 featured Miss America 1951, Yolande Betbeze, wearing a cocktail dress "made of 'Everglaze' Clarkia over diamont studded slip."[61] Another of Wilkens's Spring 1951 designs for America's Elegantes sponsored by Reich-Goldfarb, a coatdress of M. & W. wrinkle-resistant cotton with a white piqué collar and a narrow bow-tie, was chosen as part of the wardrobe for 1951 Maid of Cotton, Miss Jeannine Holland. The Maid of Cotton was essentially an ambassador for the American cotton industry, and her role included encouraging increased cotton production.[62]

Wilkens also partnered with well-known accessories manufacturers to create the perfect accessories for her garments of this period. Stetson, now best known for cowboy hats, produced non-Western-wear styles for both men and women in the mid-twentieth-century. For example, in 1947 Stetson's millinery line for women included a bright green "Stetsonian" with black net veiling and a range of hats priced from $6.95.[63] Wilkens styled hats from Stetson for her line.[64]

Wilkens also worked with ballet-shoe manufacturer Capezio to create shoes that matched a specific dress. Capezio's New York head Ben Sommers had seized on the opportunity created by wartime shoe rationing to position Capezio as a partner for New York fashion designers. Ballet slippers were not subject to rationing as regular shoes were during the war, so Capezio began stocking unusual colors and sizes and covering slippers in patterned fabrics to match a ready-to-wear designer's line. Capezio then continued making slippers and pumps for street wear after the war.[65] For Spring 1951, Wilkens designed a "dotted dance dress of Wedgwood blue and white silk over pleated organdy petticoat," and Capezio supplied matching dotted pumps.[66] An extant strapless evening dress, in red with similar white polka dots, may also date from 1951 (Plates 25, 26).

Wilkens's Fall 1951 collection—"sponsored" by Reich-Goldfarb, according to newspaper reports—was shown in June at the Park Lane Hotel on Central Park South, where she and her family lived. With this collection, Wilkens branched out further, introducing a second line with misses sizes and styling.[67] Fashion historian David E. (Ned) Lazaro has noted that the Emily Wilkens Fall 1951 and Spring 1953 collections were among the higher quality ready-to-wear offerings advertised to the Smith College community by Massachusetts custom designer and specialty shop Angotti.[68]

An extant navy short-sleeved afternoon/cocktail dress is probably from Wilkens's work with Reich-Goldfarb (Plate 20). This dress has historicizing design components that recall mid-nineteenth-century fashion, including an attached bertha-style collar, v-shaped waistline, and a pleated waistband. The pleating, while not as deep and luxurious as nineteenth-century cartridge pleating, is still an interesting appropriation of nineteenth-century construction technique and shows Wilkens's expression of historicism in the 1950s as more integral to the garment rather than the pastiche of passementerie she sometimes used in the 1940s.

A black, strapless, "ballerina-length" evening dress is also probably from Wilkens's Fall 1951 Reich-Goldfarb collection (Plate 27). This dress features a swath of velvet around the waistband, and the skirt and crumb-catcher section of the bodice are made in a fabric of wide stripes. The fabric alternates sheer and opaque stripes so that in the sheer sections a cream underlayer shows through the black. These wide black stripes bring to mind striped textiles fashionable in the 1860s.[69]

A glen plaid cotton suit with a slim skirt and a boxy short jacket of the style Wilkens termed a "toppit" was featured in the spring 1952 edition of *Dodge News*.[70] In April 1952, at a meeting of the Knitted Fabrics Institute at the Pierre Hotel in New York, Wilkens participated as a judge on a panel that also included Claire McCardell and Carolyn Schnurer, evaluating a student design competition that utilized cotton knits.[71]

Wilkens maintained her relationship with the Bonwit Teller specialty store, and for Fall/Winter 1953 she did an exclusive collection of juniors clothes for them, which included dresses and coats.[72] The collection was first presented in a fashion show on the Starlight Roof of the Waldorf-Astoria Hotel on September 9.[73] The collection was then sold in Bonwit's branch locations in Chicago, Boston, Cleveland, and White Plains, as well as in the main New York City store.[74]

Also in 1953, Wilkens again used the Patterns of the *Times* American Designer Series of home sewing patterns as a promotional vehicle for her main line of designs for Bonwit Teller (Fig. 22).[75] The patterns were for separates, one with a full skirt and off-the-shoulder blouse, the other a suit of "topper box jacket" and slim sheath skirt. Wilkens designed the fuller skirt pattern with a historicizing ball-fringe trim and also imagined it trimmed with the wearer's name; the pattern illustration shows "Emily" adorning the skirt in Wilkens's handwriting with her signature flower dotting the *i*. The skirt pattern called for three and three-eighths yards of fabric in the largest size, a juniors size seventeen (assuming a thirty-five-inch width fabric without nap). Extra volume for the skirt was achieved through the use of two-inch crinoline at the skirt hem; this construction technique was also used in Wilkens's ready-to-wear, such as the extant red-and-white polka-dot dress (Plate 26).

A surviving notebook of Wilkens's sketches and swatches from the Fall/Winter 1953 collection for Bonwit Teller shows a bit about how Wilkens worked, thought, and communicated with the production team. Each sketch is signed and dated (Fall 1953) by Wilkens in the lower right-hand corner. Her personal signature now incorporates the Emily Wilkens signature flower as the dot over her letter *i* (Plate 28).

Figure 43. Emily Wilkens for Bonwit Teller. Evening dress. Fashion sketch number 130 with swatch. Fall 1953. Courtesy of Hugh Wilkens Levey and Jane Wilkens Michael.

As in the 1946 sketches in the collection of the Brooklyn Museum, each design has a reference number in the top right-hand corner. The top left-hand corner of each sketch is labeled, sometimes with a category such as "suit" but more often with the correct time of day for the garment to be worn: day, afternoon, or evening (Fig. 43). The etiquette of a garment's appropriateness to time and place was of utmost importance to Wilkens;

EVENING

132

ROUNDED TOP

ZIP BACK

SEPERATE
SHAWL
WORN
AS
APRON

EMBROIDERED
APRON

BROAD CLOTH

TIE
IN
BACK

FRINGE

TAPERED
SHEATH
UNDERNEATH

Emily Wilkens
Fall 1953

Figure 44. Emily Wilkens for Bonwit Teller. Evening dress with embroidered apron. Fashion sketch number 132 with swatch. Fall 1953. Courtesy of Hugh Wilkens Levey and Jane Wilkens Michael.

these labels demonstrate that she kept such considerations in mind even as she was designing, just as she consistently urged her clients and readers to organize their wardrobes this way.[76]

Unlike the 1946 sketches, which were finished in bright watercolor, the 1953 Bonwit Teller sketches are copies left in black and white, probably from pencil and charcoal-pencil originals. One major difference between the sketches in this notebook and those from 1946 is the inclusion of construction notations in the later sketches. Garments are labeled with notes as to pocket placement, type of back fastening, sleeve construction, and other details that might not be clear in the sketch (Plate 29). While Wilkens was running her own Emily Wilkens Young Originals business and more directly involved with the production of the garments, she may not have needed to include this type of information on her sketches. But in her collections under the auspices of Bonwit Teller she was probably somewhat removed from the manufacturing of the garments, and therefore the sketches had to communicate information she previously could have conveyed in person. The 1953 sketches also sometimes include back views (Fig. 44) or views of a blouse hidden by a jacket in the main sketch (Plate 30).

Some elements of Wilkens's Fall/Winter 1953 collection for Bonwit Teller strike a note more modern than historicizing. The understatement of black coats with linings of paisley and matching cravat has more in common with Chanel's hidden-luxury aesthetic (and practice of matching jacket linings to blouses) than with the nineteenth century's fashionable swathes of paisley shawls (Plates 29, 31).[77] Wilkens did explicitly admire elements of simplicity and modernism in Chanel's style: "Many chic women have found a dress that's perfect and use the basic style for all seasons," Wilkens declared. "Madame Chanel is one example; her Chanel suit, in various fabrics, does round-the-clock duty."[78] The paisley cravat fabric and black broadcloth swatched in the sketch book were used in actual production, as seen in a Bonwit Teller ad for the collection (Fig. 45—showing the cravat of sketch 318 with the suit of sketch 101), and were described in the *New York Times*: "A refreshing note in the suits . . . was the use of cotton paisley in linings and ascot scarfs [*sic*]."[79]

One surviving example from Wilkens's Fall/Winter 1953 Bonwit Teller collection is a red day coat (Plate 32). This was look 115 (later changed to 104) from her book of sketches, and the sketch includes swatches of both the coat and trim fabric (Plate 33). The *New York Times* described this coat: "The Wilkens coats are fitted and have moderately flared skirts. Double-breasted and of red fleece, one was piped in black satin and fastened with black satin buttons."[80] Wilkens notes on the sketch that the red material was to come from the fabric company Jasco, and styles the coat with a black satin beret to match the buttons and trim. Jasco New York

BONWIT TELLER

Emily Wilkens,

Bonwit's own designer

for Young Charmers,

does a new

fall collection

Black wool broadcloth suit . . .
simple, shaped, with a paisley
printed cotton lining and scarf.
Also worsted flannel 79.95
Black wool broadcloth coat . . .
the princess bell silhouette
with a big kitten bow, lined
with Milium 89.95 Both in
junior sizes 7 to 15. Please,
no mail or telephone orders.
Our exclusives in New York
Chicago Boston Cleveland
White Plains

Figure 45. Bonwit Teller advertisement. Fall 1953.

LLC, founded in 1946, still sells its signature line of knits made in the United States.[81]

The label for the red coat contains the words "Bonwit Teller" in a bold black typeface that dominates the design, with "Emily Wilkens" in a lighter, red script off to the side (Plate 34). Wilkens's signature flower does not appear. The label symbolizes what had happened for Wilkens professionally, from being a named designer with her own company to doing a project for a specialty store.

The red coat does not contain a size label, but it does contain the Coat and Suit Industry National Recovery Board's consumer protection label, which certifies that the garment was "Manufactured Under Fair Labor Standards." The board, a self-governing body for that segment of the American fashion industry, was a product of the Great Depression, organized by member manufacturers in 1935 to carry on New Deal–style competition and labor policies after Franklin D. Roosevelt's National Recovery Administration was struck down as unconstitutional.[82] Manufacturing of Wilkens's designs for Bonwit Teller was probably subcontracted out to different factories, depending on the type of garment to be produced. Although this coat was made by a company that adhered to National Coat and Suit Recovery Board policies, the evening dresses would likely have been produced by manufacturers not bound to these rules.

A small group of sketches in the back of the notebook seems to have been used to work out the order of a fashion show—perhaps even the initial presentation of the collection. In this section, circled numbers in red ink paired with women's names tell the order of the show, and which ensemble would be worn by which model: Barbara, Gale, Shirley, and Pat.

The last fashion design by Wilkens to receive coverage in *Vogue* magazine was a navy wool dress illustrated by René Bouché for the February 15, 1954, issue.[83] This dress was advertised by Bonwit Teller: "Bonwit's Young Charmers in navy wool by our own Emily Wilkens . . . The spring mood is here with our exclusive new navy wool series. . . . Sizes 5 to 15, also in gray, 49.95, Junior Dresses, Young Seventh Floor."[84] Spring 1954 also saw Wilkens creating a line at similar price points under the auspices of J. L. F. Originals; these clothes were not exclusively sold at Bonwit Teller but also available at stores such as Garfinckel's in Washington, D.C.[85]

Interestingly, in what may have been Wilkens's last fashion collection, she worked with a different store and targeted yet another niche sizing group: what would later be called "petites." A September 1955 Lord & Taylor advertisement for a faux-fur mantle with black, brown, or beige exterior and a leopard-print lining declared, "Emily Wilkens designs this urbane little elegance for the 5'4" figure . . ."[86] This venture seems to mark the end of Wilkens's fashion-design career, but it did not represent the end of her involvement with the fashion industry. Wilkens would change her focus to beauty, honing her skills as a writer and motivational speaker.

Another of Wilkens's projects in the 1950s was authoring a series of articles on "teenage success" in the self-help home-study course *The Charming Woman.*[87] Wilkens shared billing in *The Charming Woman* (edited by Helen Fraser of the Barbizon School of Modeling) with beauty moguls Charles Revson and Helena Rubinstein, milliner Mr. John, fashion designer Maurice Rentner, and opera singer Lily Pons. Wilkens's articles contain many of the same points as *Here's Looking at . . . You!*, but introduce a less-gimmick-driven writing style.[88]

Wilkens worked hard to balance her professional and personal life, but even the sympathetic fashion journalist Virginia Pope remarked in the 1950s, "From time to time in the last few years, Emily has done a vanishing act."[89] Pope went on to say that Wilkens's absences from the fashion sphere were "quite understandable" due to the demands of marriage and family, but nevertheless, it was noticed and drew comment. In her struggle to express herself through her work while at the same time fulfilling the roles of wife and mother, Wilkens is emblematic of the tensions in women's status in the early post–World War II period.

B y the 1960s, when Emily Wilkens was in her forties, she had ended her fashion-design career, increasingly shifting her focus to health and beauty (Fig. 46). Perhaps the pursuit of beauty became of more primary interest to her as she herself began the process of aging away from the youthful ideal body upon which her fashion designs were premised. She would later write,

> It is true that a beautiful woman's early years do tend to be gloriously insouciant; growing old is something that happens to OTHER people. Then, suddenly, she is ambushed by time. Something happens—it may be the trauma of bearing her first child, or her second. It may be a divorce. In one awful, panicky moment, she is made to understand she is no longer a girl.[1]

Wilkens began to rebuild her public persona—in early-twenty-first-century jargon, to "rebrand" herself—as a general beauty expert, rather than primarily a fashion designer. It was in many ways a natural progression, as Wilkens was already living out the principles and tips

CHAPTER NINE

A New You

Figure 46. Emily Wilkens,
early 1960s. Courtesy of
Hugh Wilkens Levey and
Jane Wilkens Michael.

she had been dispensing since the publication of *Here's Looking at . . . You!*

Healthy eating was a major part of Wilkens's beauty regimen. Journalist Elizabeth Gage wrote, "If Emily Wilkens invites you in for tea this
afternoon, be prepared to find a bowl of honey instead of sugar on the
tea service and to be offered sesame seed cookies and a glass a freshly
squeezed carrot and apple juice."[2] Wilkens's children confirm that she
was an early enthusiast for health foods. Both Jane and Hugh recall their
mother serving them glasses of iron-rich but disgusting liver juice. Jane
recalls that beneath one window of their East River apartment there was
a flourishing tree, apparently fertilized by the liver juice the children sur-
reptitiously dumped out the window.[3]

Wilkens's largest project of the 1960s was creating the Workshop in
External Impressions at the Fashion Institute of Technology (FIT) in
New York City. For several years she personally conducted these makeover classes, coaching aspiring designers on how to achieve her signature
"bandbox" look as a key to furthering their fashion-industry careers (Fig.
47).

Figure 47. Emily
Wilkens teaching at FIT
in the 1960s. Courte-
sy of Hugh Wilkens
Levey and Jane Wilkens
Michael.

Wilkens's long-term involvement with FIT would include serving as a
member of the board of the Educational Foundation for the Fashion Industries and as a trustee of the institute (1966–1976).[4] She appears in the
FIT course catalogue for the first time in the 1963–1965 edition, which
lists her as a lecturer-consultant and gives the following biographical
blurb: "Emily Wilkens—External Impressions Workshop. Pratt Institute;
School of Fine and Applied Arts; authority in field of design and personal
appearance; author, lecturer on tour and television."[5] Wilkens is listed as a
lecturer-consultant in the catalogue for the following school year (1965–
1967) as well, with a slightly more succinct blurb, which describes her
simply as "Author, lecturer, and television speaker."[6] However, unlike other
well-known lecturer-consultants such as textile designer Pola Stout and
fashion journalist Virginia Pope, Wilkens's photograph does not appear
in the FIT yearbook.[7]

The External Impressions Workshop was Wilkens's opportunity to
bring to life her youthful ideal of the body in a way that went beyond
designing clothes for teenagers. Now, through her workshops, she was

able to impress her ideal of beauty directly upon the rising generation of fashion designers and others in the fashion industry. Part makeover and part charm school, the External Impressions Workshop was offered to all FIT freshmen in the mid-1960s. Wilkens's daughter, Jane, recalls that the girls in the External Impressions Workshop had "before and after" photographs taken.[8] In the course, Wilkens covered topics ranging from grooming to poise to wardrobe coordination. She served as her own muse for these course topics, writing in 1965, for example, "My 'barebones' basic wardrobe is built around different shadings of beige. . . . My dark color is black—which agrees with beige. Blue-green also compliments my coloring, but I save it for accents, or for casual or formal wear. . . ."

In 1965, the FIT Board of Trustees established the Emily Wilkens Chair in External Impressions "for the further development of a program in External Impressions. It honors Miss Wilkens for her assistance and counsel in founding a program which fostered self-evaluation and self-improvement as steps towards social maturity."[9] In 1965, Wilkens wrote a second book, *A New You: The Art of Good Grooming*, which aimed to make the course material of the External Impressions Workshop available to teenagers across the United States.[10]

Wilkens designed a prototype for a home makeover/beauty kit to go along with *A New You*. Although it was never manufactured, the prototype survives and is still in the collection of her family (Plate 35). The outside of the package is pink-and-white stripes, with a label made to look like mailing envelope, and the words "A New You/Emily Wilkens/She Cares!" (Plate 36). The design implies that the kit is a personal note from Wilkens to the teen purchaser and reinforces the same wise, caring "big-sister" image that Wilkens had relied on in selling her teen clothing in the 1940s.

The package design of pink-and-white stripes, with her name, and an envelope sealed with a pink heart motif, was created in collaboration with the visual merchandiser Lester Gaba, who was a friend of Wilkens'.[11] Gaba, best known for his mannequin design (including the "celebrity" mannequin, Cynthia) and soap carving, had also designed commercially available soaps, so he offered experience in the mass-market beauty industry.[12]

Inside, the package would have contained makeup divided into three different categories: Basic, Basic Plus, and Special Effects. Basic makeup included three foundations, "brush on brow," mascara, blush, "A New You

Lip Glacé," and "A New You Lip Glow." Basic Makeup Plus added eyeliner and brush, translucent powder, lip pencil and brush, "Shadow-out Cream," and "Sheen." Special Effects contained eye contouring, face contouring, and "Luscious Lashes," each in an individual box with the envelope and heart seal motif and the "Emily Wilkens—She cares" motto.

Just as Wilkens's fashion-show commentary for her 1940s teen clothing helped teenagers understand the times of day and types of activities for which a particular garment was designed, the *A New You* kit would have emphasized similarly appropriate makeup. The Basic and Basic Plus cosmetics are shown on a chart insert beside a girl in a day dress (Plate 37). The Special Effects makeup is illustrated by a girl in evening dress, with a tuxedo-clad male admirer on each side. The message is clear—judicious use of the right beauty products will help a young woman achieve popularity with and the love of the opposite sex (underlined by the repeated pink hearts). However, the *A New You* makeover-kit project did not come to fruition.

Another idea that was ultimately shelved was a proposed younger fashion line, "Up in Janie's Room," designed by Wilkens and her daughter Jane. When Jane was once heard to say "I hope it works out," she was admonished by Lester Gaba to say instead "It *will* work out."[13] This type of determination paired with creativity seems to be one of the keys to success in the fashion industry, both in the twentieth century and the twenty-first. Wilkens continued to have ample ideas for new projects throughout her career.

By the mid-1960s, Wilkens was ready to articulate her beliefs about feminism and the way work and family balance had played out in her own life. On one hand, she embraced some tenets of second-wave feminism, including the idea that being a homemaker could be dull. In 1965, she wrote,

> In this day and age, more and more women are finding happiness and fulfillment in interesting, fruitful careers.... The happy housewife myth was created in part, at least, by advertisers who were delighted to see sales going up as these supposedly happy women bought gadget after gadget in the hopes that an automatic potato peeler would chase away the boredom that filled their lives.[14]

Wilkens advocated a have-it-all type of feminism, combining marriage and family. She seems to have been describing her own hopes and experiences of being a "working mother" when she asserted that children

> love and respect a mother who doesn't cling to them and live through them because she has no life of her own. It isn't easy to combine marriage and a career—there are all kinds of conflicts and problems. Nurses and housekeepers are expensive; you feel guilty sometimes; you get tired. . . . If you plan carefully, you can find a way to juggle things during your children's early years, until you are free to pursue the career of your choice.[15]

Wilkens's feminist perspective is that of a middle-class woman who works for enjoyment and fulfillment; she does not speak to the concerns of working-class or poor women, for whom employment above all meant a paycheck. With regard to personal relationships she is not a feminist at all, encouraging teenage girls to flatter the male ego as an effective means of building a relationship.[16] Unlike many feminists of the 1960s, she did not believe that a woman should have to minimize her interest in beauty or act like a man. However, her brand of feminism that is not anti-femininity does in some ways foreshadow aspects of third-wave feminism, as she believed a woman could be both attractive and successful at the same time.

In the 1969–1970 FIT Course Catalogue, the External Impressions Workshop is described as consisting of "[r]egular sessions conducted on a voluntary basis for freshmen."[17] Dramatic changes had occurred in the "external impression" that American teenagers were now choosing to present to the world. Reviewing the FIT *Portfolio* yearbooks over the course of the 1960s and 1970s, it is interesting to see shorter, set hairdos in the style of Kenneth Battelle give way to long, straight, hippie-style hair. In the design of the *Portfolio* yearbook one can see the student attitude toward "establishment authority" change, as faculty member photos go from individual portraits to group snapshots and the listing of administrative bodies such the FIT Board of Directors is completely dropped.[18]

Perhaps Wilkens sensed that these changes were on the way even in 1963 and sought to forestall the breakdown and bridge the generation gap through her External Impressions Workshops, giving creative teenagers

Figure 48. Emily Wilkens with Dr. Ana Aslan of the Bucharest Geriatrics Institute. Wilkens profiled Aslan's anti-aging clinic and Gerovital injections in her spa books. Courtesy of Hugh Wilkens Levey and Jane Wilkens Michael.

the practical cues necessary to succeed in an appearance-driven industry. But by 1970, a charm-school-type course was as out of favor as Wilkens's earlier vision of well-scrubbed, well-groomed, well-dressed teenage girls. The Emily Wilkens Chair in External Impressions continues to be listed on FIT's website as an honorary chair, but the External Impressions Workshop faded away and is no longer mentioned in course catalogues after 1971.[19]

The unwashed hippie look must have been incredibly distasteful to Wilkens's aesthetic. However, Wilkens proved herself not just an able identifier of trends, but also someone who knew when to move on (perhaps an even rarer trait). Ever inventive, Wilkens changed her audience from teenagers to adult spa and health enthusiasts, recognizing this as an up-and-coming market for the wellness-based beauty she had been advocating since the 1940s (Fig. 48).

Wilkens wrote, "[F]ormerly, it WAS only women of wealth and leisure

Figure 49. Emily Wilkens became a columnist for King Features Syndicate in the late 1960s. Author's collection.

who were interested in spas. But now everybody is interested—men and women, young and old—and just about anybody can find a spa within a suitable price range."[20] Just as she had recognized the burgeoning teen market in the 1940s, Wilkens showed a consistent ability to capitalize on her own interests and talents by applying them to cultural trends—she had an instinct not only for fashion in the clothing sense but for identifying emerging appearance-related fashions in a variety of areas.

By the late sixties, Wilkens had also gone back to work for King Features Syndicate—this time as a columnist rather than a fashion artist (Fig. 49). Wilkens's syndicated column, titled "A New You," addressed many of the same issues as her book of that name, including diet and nutrition, but was geared to a broader audience, embracing male and female readers of all ages.[21] The column appeared three times per week, with Monday's column featuring celebrity interviews, Wednesday's column devoted to beauty and etiquette questions and answers, and Friday's column focusing on diet and exercise.[22] She would continue this work into the nineteen-eighties.[23]

The 1970s brought major changes in Wilkens's personal life. On August 10, 1970, Wilkens's husband of over twenty years, Judge Irving L. Levey, passed away in Italy.[24] Three years later, the newspaper write-up of her son Hugh's wedding listed her as Mrs. Justin Kingson, and noted that she still wrote her King Features syndicated column as Emily Wilkens (Fig. 50).[25] A business letter addressed to her as Ms. Emily Wilkens-Bass in August 1979 shows that by then she had remarried yet again and was living in Chicago.[26]

Throughout the 1970s, Wilkens continued to travel as a guest lecturer at clubs across the country, demonstrating the natural-product-based beauty tips she had garnered from various spas (such as lemon juice to lighten elbows) by making and applying her formulas during the lectures.[27]

In 1976, Wilkens published *Secrets from the Super Spas*, a book that details her home spa tips as well as descriptions of well-known spas all over the world.[28] In promoting her book, Wilkens embarked on a whirlwind publicity tour of the United States, sponsored by hair-care products manufacturer Clairol. Wilkens carefully added to her scrapbook a photocopy of her daily schedule from a stop in Los Angeles, with a note, "Typical schedule I do [in] each city." For January 26, 1977, for example, Wilkens started her day with an 8 a.m. television interview on *A.M. Los Angeles* with Regis Philbin. At 10:30 a.m., she taped a radio segment for broadcast in fifteen cities. At noon she attended a press lunch at the Brown Derby restaurant in Hollywood before flying on to San Francisco at 5 p.m. A typewritten note at the end of the day's schedule of "interviews awaiting confirmation" listed another radio program and *Playgirl* magazine.[29]

Another of Wilkens's projects in conjunction with Clairol was a television program. Long before reality television crowded the schedule, Wilkens had her own television makeover show sponsored by Clairol, called *The Magic Mirror*. The tagline for the program was "Revealing Fashion, Beauty, and Glamour Secrets to Enchant Women Everywhere." Singer Johnny Desmond was her co-host.[30]

Secrets from the Super Spas was so successful that Wilkens went on to release an updated edition, *More Secrets from the Super Spas*, in 1983.[31] In the 1980s, Wilkens stepped back from an active role on the FIT Board of Trustees and was named a trustee emerita in 1982.[32]

In 1991, Wilkens, in her early seventies, was diagnosed with dementia. She spent the last years of her life at the Hebrew Home for the Aged, in Riverdale, New York.[33]

Wilkens's contribution to American fashion, and specifically American sportswear, was acknowledged in 1998, when two of her Spring/Summer 1945 Emily Wilkens Young Originals garments were featured in *American Ingenuity*, an exhibition that ran from April through August at the Costume Institute Metropolitan Museum of Art. The garments displayed in the exhibit were part of a group of nine Emily Wilkens Young Originals ensembles Wilkens had donated to the museum over the course of 1945. Wilkens's donation supported the institution she utilized for historic garment research and may also represent a conscious effort toward legacy-building.

The Wilkens items included in the *American Ingenuity* exhibition were a playsuit and an evening dress, both of Everfast striped cotton. These garments were grouped in a thematic section titled "Adapting" that considered sportswear as a kind of rational dress, freeing women from discomfort and unnecessary expense. In this section, Wilkens's designs were shown alongside those of Claire McCardell, Tina Leser, and Carolyn Schnurer—colleagues with whom she had shared honors in the 1940s and 1950s. Curator Richard Martin thanked his friend Emily Wilkens in the exhibition catalogue acknowledgments, writing that it was a privilege to know her. In the text he praised Wilkens's "charming, cultivated dresses for the young."[34]

Figure 50. Emily Wilkens, far left, with husband Justin Kingson seated to her right at a 1970s event. Courtesy of Hugh Wilkens Levey and Jane Wilkens Michael.

Wilkens died on December 2, 2000, just two years after her work was celebrated in *American Ingenuity*.[35] Echoes of her legacy can be seen in the dominance of youth as the ideal of beauty; in teenagers' agency in shaping culture; in retailers' consciousness of and desire to appeal to teen consumers with products specifically for them; and in many young designers' ambitions to start their own companies rather than "paying their dues" in someone else's firm.

There are creative individuals who have a clear vision and who contribute to the world just by being themselves; Emily Wilkens was one of those people. Wilkens wrote in 1948, "The same principle applies either to the six-year-old or the sixty-year-old—simplicity, good grooming, and good taste."[36] From her personality-driven dresses for Hollywood children in the early 1940s, to her ready-to-wear for teenagers, to her spa and beauty writing for adults in the 1980s, Wilkens was true to her ideals of beauty throughout her life and career.

INTRODUCTION

1. Eleanor Lambert, *World of Fashion* (New York & London: R. R. Bowker, 1976), 284.

CHAPTER 1

1. Jane Wilkens Michael, e-mail to author, 8 April 2013.
2. "Bernard Wilkens, A Psychiatrist, 43," *New York Times*, 29 July 1966; Ginia Bellafante, "Emily Wilkens, 83, Designer Who Dressed Girls Like Girls," *New York Times*, 6 December 2000; Jane Wilkens Michael, interview by author, 22 March 2012; Michael Lucks, "Genealogy of Lucks, Kai and Related Families: Emily Ann Wilkens" http://www.mlucks.com/genealogy/lucks/descend.php?personID=I3310& tree=6, accessed 21 March 2012.
3. Hasia Diner, "American Jewish Identity and the Garment Industry," in Gabriel M. Goldstein and Elizabeth Greenberg, eds., *A Perfect Fit: The Garment Industry and American Jewry, 1860–1960* (Lubbock: Texas Tech University Press and Yeshiva University Museum, 2012), 29.
4. Bellafante, "Emily Wilkens"; Michael interview, 22 March 2012. One family genealogist states that the 1930 census lists Emily's birthplace as New York; however, closer family members give Hartford as Emily's birthplace. Lucks, "Genealogy of Lucks."
5. Jane Wilkens Michael, interview by author, 9 April 2012.
6. Beryl Williams, *Fashion Is Our Business* (Philadelphia: J. B. Lippincott, 1945), 36.

7. Ibid., 35.

8. Eleanor Lambert, "Emily Wilkens Biography" press release, the Metropolitan Museum of Art, Costume Institute Library, vertical files, 1. ocl 201490998.

9. Michael interview, 22 March 2012.

10. Emily Wilkens, "A New You" column, "Cellular Therapy: A Way to Recapture Lost Youth," *The Hartford Courant*, 9 January 1975.

11. Mrs. Christine Frederick, *Selling Mrs. Consumer* (New York: The Business Bourse, 1929), 36.

12. Kelly Schrum, *Some Wore Bobby Sox: The Emergence of Teenage Girls' Culture, 1920–1945* (New York: Palgrave-Macmillan, 2004), 79–80.

13. Emily Wilkens, *More Secrets from the Super Spas* (New York: Dembner, 1983), 22; Emily Wilkens, *Secrets from the Super Spas* (New York: Grosset & Dunlap, 1976), 22.

14. Williams, *Fashion Is Our Business*, 35.

15. Emily Wilkens, *Here's Looking at . . . You!* ed. Dorothy Roe Lewis (New York: G. P. Putnam's Sons, 1948), 2, 36, 37; Williams, *Fashion Is Our Business*, 35.

16. Wilkens, *More Secrets*, 133. In her first spa book, she refers to the Swiss governess, but it is unclear whether the governess is remembered from her own childhood or was a caregiver for Emily Wilkens's children. In the revised edition, the statement is edited to reflect a personal memory of Wilkens's childhood. Wilkens, *Secrets*, 120.

17. Wilkens, *Here's Looking*, 2.

18. Williams, *Fashion Is Our Business*, 36.

19. Wilkens, *Here's Looking*, 2; Williams, *Fashion Is Our Business*, 36.

20. Lambert, "Emily Wilkens Biography," 1.

21. Ibid.

22. Jane Wilkens Michael, "Estée!" *Town and Country* [no date], 82.

23. Betty Barrett, "Spa-Hopper Will Divulge How to Set Up Beauty Routine," *The Hartford Courant*, 26 August 1976.

24. According to both Beryl Williams and Emily's daughter, Jane, she may have actually gotten into Smith but stymied her family by choosing art school instead. Michael interview, 22 March 2012; Williams, *Fashion Is Our Business*, 38, 42; Jessie Stuart, *The American Fashion Industry* (Boston: Simmons College, 1951), 63.

25. Williams, *Fashion Is Our Business*, 38, 42; Stuart, *American Fashion Industry*, 63; Edith Radom, "Teenagers Glamourized by Fashions Designed Exclusively for Them," *The Hartford Courant Magazine*, 16 April 1944.

26. Margaretta Byers, *Help Wanted—Female* (New York: Julian Messner, 1941), 370; Bellafante, "Emily Wilkens"; Williams, *Fashion Is Our Business*, 39.

27. Michael interview, 22 March 2012; Williams, *Fashion Is Our Business*, 37.

28. Williams, *Fashion Is Our Business*, 51.

29. Pratt Institute, *Prattonia* yearbook (Brooklyn, NY: Pratt Institute, 1938), 51.

30. Office of the Registrar, Pratt Institute, e-mail to author, dated 19 April 2013; Bellafante, "Emily Wilkens"; Williams, *Fashion Is Our Business*, 39.

31. Bellafante, "Emily Wilkens."

32. Byers, *Help Wanted—Female*, 220.

33. Williams, *Fashion Is Our Business*, 40.

34. Lambert, "Emily Wilkens Biography," 1; Virginia Pope, "Designer's Career a Storybook One," *New York Times,* 1 September 1945.

35. Bernice Gertrude Chambers, ed., *Keys to a Fashion Career* (New York: McGraw-Hill, 1946), 87.

36. Williams, *Fashion Is Our Business*, 43–44; Chambers, *Keys,* 87.

37. Lady [Lucy Christiana] Duff Gordon, *Discretions and Indiscretions* (London: Jarrolds, 1932), 41–42.

38. Wilkens, *Here's Looking*, 39; Williams, *Fashion Is Our Business*, 44.

39. Wilkens, *Here's Looking*, 39.

40. Ibid., 39–40.

41. American Girl, "American Girl Clothing; Matching in style – and Spirit," http://store.americangirl.com/agshop/static/clothing.jsp, accessed 5 February 5, 2013.

42. Bernice G. Chambers, *Fashion Fundamentals* (Englewood Cliffs, NJ: Prentice-Hall, 1947), 28. This is an interesting parallel with Eleanor Estes' 1944 children's book, *The Hundred Dresses*, in which the bullied character Wanda Petronski's prize-winning dress illustrations show her classmates in the designs. It is interesting to speculate whether Estes—who, like Wilkens, was from Connecticut—may have been inspired by media coverage of Emily Wilkens's childrenswear sketches to develop an uplifting ending for her poignant novel. Eleanor Estes, *The Hundred Dresses* (New York: Harcourt, 1944), 78–79.

43. Chambers, *Keys*, 86.

44. Byers, *Help Wanted—Female*, 172.

45. Sara Little, "Young America's Favorite Dress Designer Lives Here," *House Beautiful*, August 1945, 60–61. In her "Girl with a Future" articles, Little (born 1917 in Manhattan and raised in Brooklyn) dealt with the issues she anticipated would be on the minds of American women in the postwar period, "modern ideas such as sharing an apartment with a roommate, decorating a home for a returning soldier, doing away with a cleaning lady, or making the best of the GI Bill." In 1948, Little would illustrate Wilkens's first book. Sara Little

(later Sara Little Turnbull after her 1965 marriage to James R. Turnbull) would go on to a long career as a designer of commercial products of all kinds, collaborating with companies such as General Mills, Corning, Procter & Gamble, and 3M. Veronique Vienne, "The Why of It All," *Metropolis Magazine*, November 2000. http://www.metropolismag.com/html/content_1100/tur.htm accessed 15 November 2007.

46. Williams, *Fashion Is Our Business*, 44, 47.

47. Ibid., 44–46.

48. Chambers, *Keys,* 87; Chambers, *Fashion Fundamentals*, 186; Lambert, "Emily Wilkens Biography," 2; Williams, *Fashion Is Our Business*, 47.

49. Saks Fifth Avenue advertisement, *New York Herald Tribune*, 20 September 1942.

50. Cora Carlyle, "Take Time for Teens," *Women's Reporter*, November 1944, n.p.

51. "'Polio Poster Girl' Here for Big Drive," *New York Times*, 14 January 1947.

CHAPTER 2

1. Wilkens, *Here's Looking,* 40; Lambert, "Emily Wilkens Biography," 2; Stuart, *American Fashion Industry*, 63.

2. Sally Benson, *Junior Miss* (New York: Random House, 1939).

3. "Broadway in Review," *Theatre Arts*, vol. xxvi, no.1 (January 1942): 9; "A Woman of Thirteen," *The New Yorker*, 29 November 1941, 39; Jerome Chodorov and Joseph Fields, *Junior Miss* (New York: Dramatists Play Service, 1942).

4. Tootsie Roll Industries, "Junior Mints Original," http://www.tootsie.com/products.php?pid=153; accessed 17 June 2011.

5. Germany declared war on the United States on December 11. J. M. Roberts, *The Penguin History of Europe* (London: Penguin, 1996), 568.

6. *The Playbill*, "*Junior Miss*," Week beginning October 18, 1942, 23.

7. "Teenagers as Customers," *Kiplinger's Personal Finance*, June 1947, 31.

8. Ready-to-wear teen sizes 10, 12, 14, 16 were intended for teenagers whose fit needs were somewhere between those of children's sizes and junior miss sizes. See discussion, infra.

9. Internet Broadway Database, "*Junior Miss* Production Credits," http://www.ibdb.com/production.asp?ID=1136 ; accessed 12 November 2007.

10. Wilkens, *Here's Looking*, 40.

11. Wilkens, *Here's Looking*, 40; Norman Krasna, *Dear Ruth* (New York: Dramatists Play Service, 1944).

12. Mary Roberts Rinehart, *Bab: A Sub-Deb* (New York: George H. Doran, 1917), 14, 20, 21, 42.

13. Ibid., 117.

14. Nancy Mitford, *Love in a Cold Climate* (New York: The Modern Library, 1994), 361.

15. Schrum, *Some Wore Bobby Sox*, 11.

16. Dorothy Hankins, "Adolescence: What Is It?", *Parents'*, April 1945, 30.

17. John Bynner, "Rethinking the Youth Phase of the Life-course: The Case for Emerging Adulthood?" *Journal of Youth Studies* 8, no. 4 (December 2005), 368.

18. Jeanne Perkins, "Emily Post," *Life*, 6 May 1946, 66.

19. Grace Palladino, *Teenagers: An American History* (New York: Basic Books, 1996), xv–xvi, 5; Schrum, *Some Wore Bobby Sox*, 3.

20. Alice Barr Grayson, *Do You Know Your Daughter?* (New York: Appleton-Century, 1944), 174. Alice Barr Grayson was the nom de plume of child psychologist Jean Schick Grossman.

21. Bynner, "Rethinking Youth Phase," 367, 369; Jeffrey Arnett, *Emerging Adulthood: The Winding Road from Late Teens through the Twenties* (Oxford: Oxford University Press, 2004), 8.

22. Bynner, "Rethinking Youth Phase," 380.

23. Ibid., 369.

24. "Clothing Fit for a Tween: Stylish Apparel, without Being Too Grown Up," *The Canadian Press*, 22 January 2010.

25. Ibid.

26. Carlyle, "Take Time for Teens."

27. Daniel Thomas Cook, *The Commodification of Childhood* (Durham & London: Duke University Press, 2004), 3.

28. Ibid., 13.

29. Ibid., 5.

30. Schrum, *Some Wore Bobby Sox*, 16.

31. Ibid., 50.

32. Benson, *Junior Miss*, 1.

33. Ibid., 12.

34. Ibid.

35. Ibid., 12–13; Chodorov and Fields, *Junior Miss*, 45.

36. Benson, *Junior Miss*, 15; Chodorov and Fields, *Junior Miss*, 8.

37. Benson, *Junior Miss*, 15; Chodorov and Fields, *Junior Miss*, 8.

38. Lambert, "Emily Wilkens Biography," 1.

39. Benson, *Junior Miss*, 16.

40. Ibid., 22.

41. Ibid.

42. Ibid., 20, 24; Chodorov and Fields, *Junior Miss*, 45.

43. Benson, *Junior Miss*, 20, 24; Chodorov and Fields, *Junior Miss*, 45.

44. Lucy Rathbone and Elizabeth Tarpley, *Fabrics and Dress* (Cambridge, MA: The Riverside Press, 1943, 159.

45. Mildred Graves Ryan, *Your Clothes and Personality*, 3rd ed. (New York: Appleton-Century-Crofts, 1949), photo insert, caption 1.

46. Schrum, *Some Wore Bobby Sox*, 60.

47. National Retail Dry Goods Association, *Twenty-Five Years of Retailing* (New York: Mullens and Tutrone, 1936), 198.

48. "*The Times* Settles the Situation on Bobby Socks," *Women's Wear Daily*, 10 March 1944.

49. Schrum, *Some Wore Bobby Sox*, 58–62.

50. Jennifer M. Mower and Elaine L. Pedersen, "'Pretty and Patriotic': Women's Consumption of Apparel During World War II," *Dress* 39, no. 1 (2013): 40.

51. Ibid., 42, 43.

52. Ibid., 43–44, 53.

53. "Problems: Teenage" column, *Parents'*, March 1945, 35.

54. Schrum, *Some Wore Bobby Sox*, 58.

55. *Junior Miss*, 1945 motion picture, opening credits (Beverly Hills, CA: Twentieth Century Fox Home Entertainment, 2012), DVD; Georganne Scheiner, *Signifying Female Adolescence: Film Representations and Fans, 1920–1950* (Westport, CT, and London: Praeger, 2000), 106, 107. Bonnie Cashin began in the ready-to-wear industry in the 1930s, then spent most of the 1940s in California, costuming about 60 Hollywood films before returning to sportswear in 1949 with a Coty-Award-winning collection for Adler and Adler. Sally Kirkland, "Sportswear for Everywhere," in Richard Martin, *All-American: A Sportswear Tradition* (New York: Fashion Institute of Technology, 1985), 40.

56. Wilkens, *Here's Looking*, 8.

57. "Broadway in Review," *Theatre Arts*, vol. xxvi, no.1 (January 1942): 14, photograph by Fred Fehl; "Broadway in Review," *Theatre Arts*, vol. xxvi, no. 6 (June 1942): 397, photograph by Lucas Pritchard.

58. "Broadway in Review," *Theatre Arts*, vol. xxvi, no.1 (January 1942): 14, photograph by Fred Fehl; "Broadway in Review," *Theatre Arts*, vol. xxvi, no. 6 (June 1942): 397, photograph by Lucas Pritchard; "Schoolgirl Walks into Theater and Comes Out with Lead in Hit Show," *Life*, 15 December 1941, 104, 109.

59. Benson, *Junior Miss*, 16; Chodorov and Fields, *Junior Miss*, 8.

60. Benson, *Junior Miss*, 120.

61. Classified Ad, *New York Times*, 11 October 1946, 48.

62. Everfast, Emily Wilkens Young Originals advertisement, *Vogue,* 1 January 1946, 31.

63. Kelley Massoni, *Fashioning Teenagers: A Cultural History of Seventeen Magazine* (Walnut Creek, CA: Left Coast Press, 2010), 55–56.

64. Advertisements, "Precision Miniatures" and "Cinema Charm Manufacturers," *Seventeen*, February 1947, 236.

65. Massoni, *Fashioning Teenagers*, 93, 183.

66. Benson, *Junior Miss*, 87.

67. Anne Fogarty, *Wife Dressing* (New York: Julian Messner, 1959), 141.

68. Bonwit Teller, "New Designer for the Teens . . . Emily Wilkens," advertisement, *New York Times*, 16 April 1944, 5; *Vogue*, 1 May 1944, 137.

CHAPTER 3

1. Chambers, *Fashion Fundamentals*, 186; "A Modern and an Old-Fashioned Girl," *New York Times*, 29 March 1944, 18.

2. Mabel Greene, "Bonwit Displays Teen-age Fashions," *New York Sun*, 29 March 1944.

3. Schrum, *Some Wore Bobby Sox*, 18.

4. *Kiplinger's*, "Teenagers as Customers," 31.

5. Ibid.

6. Sheryl Farnan Leipzig, Jean L. Parsons, and Jane Farrell Beck, "It is a Profession that is New Unlimited and Rich: Promotion of the American Designer in the 1930s," *Dress* (2008–2009), 39, citing David M. Kennedy, *Freedom from Fear* (New York: Oxford University Press, 1999), 164; Sara Pennoyer, *Polly Tucker: Merchant* (New York: Dodd, Meade and Co., 1937), 224.

7. Kirkland, "Sportswear for Everywhere," 36; Kohle Yohannan and Nancy Nolf, *Claire McCardell: Redefining Modernism* (New York: Abrams, 1998), 41.

8. *Kiplinger's*, "Teenagers as Customers," 33.

9. "Junior Miss," *Life*, 19 October 1942, 80.

10. Williams, *Fashion Is Our Business*, 48.

11. Wilkens, *Here's Looking*, 40.

12. "Junior Fashions," *Vogue*, 1 June 1944, 145.

13. Williams, *Fashion Is Our Business*, 46–49.

14. Ibid., 48–49.

15. Massoni, *Fashioning Teenagers*, 81–107.

16. Rebecca Arnold, *The American Look: Fashion, Sportswear and the Image of Women in 1930s and 1940s New York* (London & New York: I.B. Tauris, 2009), 142.

17. Caroline Rennolds Milbank, *New York Fashion: The Evolution of American Style* (New York: Harry N. Abrams, 1989), 133.

18. Geraldine Howell, *Wartime Fashion: From Haute Couture to Homemade, 1939–1945* (London: Berg, 2012), 85, 89, 141.

19. Chambers, *Keys*, 87–88.

20. Michael interview, 22 March 2012.

21. Williams, *Fashion Is Our Business*, 48–49; "Junior Fashions," *Vogue*, 1 June 1944, 144. Unfortunately, I have not been able to discover any written contracts or other documentation as to the specifics of the partnership arrangement, such as how profits would have been divided.

22. Carlyle, "Take Time for Teens"; *Sheldon's Manufacturing (Cutting Up) Trade*, 44th ed. (New York: J. S. Phelon & Co., 1940), 72; Williams, *Fashion Is Our Business*, 48–49. "Chubby" girls sizes were half sizes, 8½ to 14 ½. See, for example, The Hecht Company's advertisement, "Dress Up—Slim Down in our 'Chubby Girl' Charmer," *Calling All Girls*, January/February 1945, 18.

23. "25 Receive Citations as Apparel Leaders," *New York Times*, 8 January 1947.

24. Michael interview, 22 March 2012.

25. Donald Albrecht, *The High Style of Dorothy Draper* (New York: Museum of the City of New York and Pointed Leaf Press, 2006), 58–67.

26. Bernice Fitz-Gibbon, *Macy's, Gimbels, and Me: How to Earn $90,000 a Year in Retail Advertising* (New York: Simon and Schuster, 1967), 234, 236.

27. Little, "Young America's Favorite," 60–61.

28. Lambert, "Emily Wilkens Biography," 3.

29. "Resort Fashions," *Life*, 14 January 1947, 76.

30. Wilkens, *New You*, 29.

31. Wilkens, *More Secrets*, 11; Wilkens, *Secrets*, 11.

32. Chambers, *Fashion Fundamentals*, 186.

33. "Teen Style Problems to be Discussed at Luncheon Meeting," *Women's Wear Daily*, 3 January 1945.

34. Grace Herrick, "High Jinks in Style," *New York Times*, 28 May 1944.

35. Tiffany Webber-Hanchett, "Dorothy Shaver: Promoter of 'The American Look,'" *Dress* (2003): 83; Leipzig, Parsons, and Beck, "New Unlimited and Rich," 32.

36. Gertrude Warburton and Jane Maxwell, *Fashion for a Living* (New York and London: McGraw-Hill, 1939), 115–16.

37. Arnold, *American Look*, 110.

38. Ibid., 136, 139, 164.

39. Ibid., 139; Lambert, "Emily Wilkens Biography," 1–2; Webber-Hanchett, "Dorothy Shaver," 83.

40. Bernadine Morris, "Norman Norell, Designer, Dies; Made 7th Ave. the Rival of Paris," *New York Times*, 26 October 1972.

41. Everfast, Emily Wilkens Young Originals advertisement, *Vogue*, 1 January 1946, 31.

42. Williams, *Fashion Is Our Business*, 48–49.

43. Florence S. Richards, *The Ready-to-Wear Industry 1900–1950* (New York: Fairchild, 1951), 29.

44. Chambers, *Keys*, 88.

45. Ibid., 284.

46. Everfast advertisement, "No Washing Instructions Needed," Women's Wear Daily, 7 March 1944.

47. "Bonwit Teller Presents Styles for Teen-Age Girls for Summer," *New York Herald Tribune*, 29 March 1944.

48. Rathbone and Tarpley, *Fabrics and Dress*, 53.

49. "Designer Prescribes Cottons for Growing Up Figures," *Cotton News*, July & August 1944, n.p. The *Cotton News* article claimed that her spring/summer collection was all cotton, but in fact it also contained Everfast rayon fabrics.

50. Fairchild Archive, Emily Wilkens Designer Scrapbook, clipping dated 17 July 1946. Features such as quilting and leg-of-mutton sleeves were a postwar privilege, not in compliance with the L-85 regulation.

51. Fairchild Archive, Emily Wilkens Designer Scrapbook, clipping dated 5 April 1945; Richard Martin, *American Ingenuity: Sportswear 1930s–1970s* (New York: The Metropolitan Museum of Art, 1988), 82–83; "Step into the Sun," *Harper's Bazaar, Junior Bazaar*, May 1945, 94.

52. Martin, *American Ingenuity*, 93.

53. Gertrude Bailey, " 'Young Originals' Click,' " *New York World-Telegram*, 29 March 1944.

54. Ponemah Mills advertisement, "Portrait of a Young Girl in a Postwar Fabric," *Harper's Bazaar*, March 1945, 133.

55. Chambers, *Fashion Fundamentals*, 265.

56. Virginia Pope, "Versatile Style Show Is Held with the New Everfast Fabrics," *New York Times*, 10 November 1944.

57. "Fashion Awards: Californian Wins Critics' Prize," *Life*, 26 February 1945, 33; Ponemah Mills advertisement, "Portrait of a Young Girl in a Postwar Fabric," *Harper's Bazaar*, March 1945, 133.

58. Steve Dunwell, *The Run of the Mill: A Pictorial Narrative of the Expansion, Dominion, Decline and Enduring Impact of the New England Textile Industry* (Boston: David R. Godine, 1978), 132, 134.

59. Ibid., 134.

60. Ibid., 147.

61. Ibid., 144.

62. "Do You Know a Soldier?" *Harper's Bazaar,* March 1945, 127.

63. Phyllis G. Tortora and Robert S. Merkel. *Fairchild's Dictionary of Textiles*, 7th ed. (New York: Fairchild, 2000), 67; Botany Worsted Mills advertisement, "Botany," *Parents'*, February 1945, 133.

64. Milliken advertisement, "Pert! Emily Wilkens's Bow-Tie Dress," *Seventeen*, February 1947, 6.

65. U.S. Patent Des.137,566, filed Feb. 24, 1944, patented March 28, 1944.

66. Stuart, *American Fashion Industry*, 29–30.

67. Ibid., 29.

68. "Dress Designers Rush for Patents," *New York Times*, 3 December 1946.

69. Stuart, *American Fashion Industry*, 29.

70. Emily Wilkens Young Originals advertisement, "Young Originals Designed by Emily Wilkens," *Women's Wear Daily*, 15 March 1944.

71. Bonwit Teller, "New Designer"; Design Patent Des. 137,566.

72. Bonwit Teller, "New Designer"; Design Patent Des. 137,563.

73. "Lace, Antique Vase, Even a Corset Give Inspiration for Hats at Show," *New York Times*, 25 October 1945. John-Frederics's millinery contribution was based on a piece of porcelain, Sally Victor's on nineteenth-century parasols, and Lilly Daché's on a Chinese headdress.

74. Fairchild Archive, Emily Wilkens Designer Scrapbook, clipping dated March 1946.

75. "Dress Designers Rush for Patents," *New York Times*, 3 December 1946.

76. See, for example, Emily Wilkens Young Originals advertisement, "Young America Comes Into Her Own," *Women's Wear Daily*, 1 March 1944. At times these ads were directly across the page from the Chalks's Vogue Girl Coat Company ads.

77. "Mother-Daughter Jury to Pass on Bonwit Showing," *Women's Wear Daily*, 27 March 1944.

78. "A Modern and an Old-Fashioned Girl," *New York Times*, 29 March 1944.

CHAPTER 4

1. Emily Wilkens, "Emily Wilkens Scoffs at Old Fashion Cliché that Women Can't Be Well Dressed Until 35," *Providence Journal*, 2 October 1950.

2. Robert Harling, *Steel Magnolias* (Garden City, NY: The Fireside Theatre, 1987), 4.

3. Wilkens, *New You*, 14.

4. Wilkens, *More Secrets*, 10; Wilkens, *Secrets*, 10.

5. Wilkens, *Here's Looking*, 2.

6. Ibid., 18.

7. Frances R. Donovan, quoting Antoinette Donnelly from the *Chicago Tribune*, 5 June 1928, in *The Saleslady* (Chicago: University of Chicago Press, 1929), 215.

8. Arnold, *American Look*, 47.

9. "Junior Fashions," *Vogue*, 15 May 1944, 100.

10. Ibid., 101.

11. Wilkens, *Here's Looking*. Dorothy Roe Lewis served as "editor" for other volumes of prescriptive literature by mid-twentieth-century American fashion designers, such as Lilly Daché's *Talking Through My Hats* (New York: Coward-McCann, 1946).

12. Howell, *Wartime Fashion*, 23–25.

13. Daché, *Talking Through My Hats*; Claire McCardell, *What Shall I Wear? The What, Where, When and How Much of Fashion* (New York: Simon and Schuster, 1956).

14. Bernice Bryant, *Future Perfect: A Guide to Personality and Popularity for the Junior Miss* (Indianapolis and New York: Bobbs-Merill, 1944).

15. Wilkens, *New You*, 18–19.

16. Ibid., 17.

17. Margueritte Harmon Bro, *Let's Talk About You* (New York: Doubleday, Doran & Co.: 1945), 92.

18. Anne Hollander, *Seeing Through Clothes* (Berkeley: University of California Press, 1993), 391–392.

19. Wilkens, *Here's Looking*, 5–6, 12; Wilkens, *New You*, 17.

20. Wilkens, *Secrets*, 6.

21. Wilkens, *Here's Looking*, 27.

22. Ibid., 29; Wilkens, *New You*, 51.

23. Wilkens, *Here's Looking*, 26–33, 36–37; Wilkens, *New You*, 48–49; Wilkens, *Secrets*, 39–42.

24. Wilkens, *Here's Looking*, 22; Wilkens, *New You*, 48.

25. Wilkens, *New You*, 74.

26. Wilkens, *Here's Looking*, 30–31; Wilkens, *New You*, 35–38, 43; Wilkens, *Secrets*, 45–60; Wilkens, *More Secrets*, 45–60.

27. Wilkens, *New You*, 34.

28. Ibid., 35; Emily Wilkens, "Ten Little Yogas," pamphlet, (New York: King Features Syndicate).

29. Wilkens, *Here's Looking*, 22–23.

30. Wilkens, *New You*, 14, 80.

31. Wilkens, *Here's Looking*, 8.

32. Wilkens, *New You*, 14.

33. Wilkens, *Here's Looking*, 18–19; Wilkens, *New You*, 85; Wilkens, *Secrets*, 14; Wilkens, *More Secrets*, 14.

34. Wilkens, *Here's Looking*, 18–19; Wilkens, *New You*, 85.
35. Wilkens, *New You*, 81.
36. Wilkens, *Secrets*, 14; Wilkens, *More Secrets*, 14.
37. Wilkens, *New You*, 114.
38. Ibid., 114, 116.
39. Ibid., 118; Wilkens, *Secrets*, 10, 37; Wilkens, *More Secrets*, 10, 37.
40. Wilkens, *New You*, 154–155.
41. Ibid., 135.
42. Ibid., 142.
43. Wilkens, *Here's Looking*, 20; Wilkens, *New You*, 28–29; Wilkens, *Secrets*, 64; Wilkens, *More Secrets*, 64.
44. Wilkens, *New You*, 30.
45. Wilkens, *Here's Looking*, 32; Wilkens, *New You*, 32; Wilkens, *Secrets*, 58; Wilkens, *More Secrets*, 58.
46. Wilkens, *New You*, 170.
47. "The 'Cheapest' Dressmaker," *Life*, 20 May 1946, 58G.
48. Wilkens, *New You*, 168.
49. Wilkens, *Here's Looking*, 70–71; Wilkens, *New You*, 176–178.
50. Wilkens, *Here's Looking*, 55; Wilkens, *New You*, 168.
51. Wilkens, *New You*, 168.
52. Wilkens, *Here's Looking*, 46; Wilkens, *New You*, 176–178, 194.
53. Wilkens, *Here's Looking*, 70–71; Wilkens, *New You*, 176–178.
54. Wilkens, *Here's Looking*, 48–49; Wilkens, *New You*, 174. Emily Wilkens's belief in the importance of a pared-down wardrobe may be one of the reasons she did not save archive examples of her own fashion designs.
55. Wilkens, *Here's Looking*, 46; Wilkens, *New You*, 194.
56. Wilkens, *Secrets*, 67; Wilkens, *More Secrets*, 67.
57. Wilkens, *New You*, 175.
58. Wilkens, *Here's Looking*, 44–45.
59. Stanley Ager, *The Butler's Guide to Running the Home and Other Graces* (New York: Clarkson Potter, 2012), 13,14, 57–65, 104–121; Wilkens, *Here's Looking*, 44, 46; Wilkens, *New You*, 191, 194; Emily Wilkens, "Reorganize Your Wardrobe in 10 Steps," *McCall's*, March 1948, 151.
60. Wilkens, *Here's Looking*, 55; Wilkens, *New You*, 170, 189.
61. Wilkens, *New You*, 189.
62. Ibid., 187.
63. Wilkens, *Here's Looking*, 39, 63.
64. Wilkens, *New You*, 189.

CHAPTER 5

1. Schrum, *Some Wore Bobby Sox*, 3–6.

2. Warburton and Maxwell, *Fashion for a Living*, 100. Gertrude Warburton was an editor for the *Butterick Fashion Magazine*, and Jane Maxwell was associate editor for the *Women's Home Companion*.

3. Schrum, *Some Wore Bobby Sox*, 45–49.

4. Ibid., 45.

5. "Teen Fashions for School—New Themes From Retailers," *Women's Wear Daily*, 5 September 1945.

6. Wilkens, *Here's Looking*, 40; Williams, *Fashion Is Our Business*, 48.

7. Williams, *Fashion Is Our Business*, 49–50.

8. "Neiman-Marcus Show Honors Teen Fashions," *Women's Wear Daily*, 12 September 1945.

9. "Kate Greenaway Styles," *Life*, 9 April 1945, 88.

10. Williams, *Fashion Is Our Business*, 49–50.

11. Phyllis G. Tortora and Keith Eubank, *Survey of Historic Costume*, 5th ed. (New York: Fairchild, 2010), 323, 345, 373, 403.

12. Bernard Rudofsky, *Are Clothes Modern?* (Chicago: Paul Theobald, 1947), 33.

13. Cook, *Commodification of Childhood*, 107.

14. Grayson, *Know Your Daughter?*, 174.

15. Ibid.

16. Chambers, *Fashion Fundamentals*, 186.

17. Andrew Bolton and Harold Koda, *Schiaparelli and Prada: Impossible Conversations* (New York: The Metropolitan Museum of Art, 2012), 23.

18. Elizabeth Burris-Meyer, *This Is Fashion* (New York and London: Harper, 1943),145; Pennoyer, *Polly Tucker*, 173–174.

19. Dilys E. Blum, *Shocking! The Art and Fashion of Elsa Schiaparelli* (New Haven and London: Philadelphia Museum of Art and Yale University Press, 2003), 154–155, 186–189; "Neiman-Marcus Show Honors Teen Fashions," *Women's Wear Daily*, 12 September 1945.

20. Blum, *Shocking!*, 244.

21. "A Modern and an Old-Fashioned Girl," *New York Times*, 29 March 1944. The law referenced here was the L-85 regulation which limited the fabric allowance for most American clothing during World War II.

22. Burris-Meyer, *This Is Fashion*, 62, 120–121.

23. "Emily Wilkens Picks Everfast Ginghams," advertisement, 1944, Fairchild Archive, Emily Wilkens Designer Scrapbook.

24. Office of Price Administration, *Retail Ceiling Prices for Certain Apparel and*

House Furnishings, Maximum Price Regulation No. 580 (Washington, D.C.: Government Printing Office, 1945), I.

25. Ibid., 22.
26. Ibid., 8.
27. *Kiplinger's*, "Teenagers as Customers," 33.
28. Harriet Eager Davis, "Work Summers for Teenagers," *Parents'*, June 1945, 30.
29. Hollander, *Seeing Through Clothes*, 388.
30. "Party Dresses," *Life*, 10 December 1945, 78–79.
31. Warburton and Maxwell, *Fashion for a Living*, 67.
32. Edith Radom, "Teenagers Glamourized."
33. "A Modern and an Old-Fashioned Girl," *New York Times*, 29 March 1944, 18.
34. Williams, *Fashion Is Our Business*, 50.
35. Burris-Meyer, *This Is Fashion*, 242.
36. Elizabeth Hawes, *Fashion is Spinach* (New York: Random House, 1938), 6.
37. Wilkens, *Here's Looking*, 7.
38. Ibid., 55; Wilkens, *New You*, 169, 189.
39. Bonwit Teller, "New Designer."
40. Grace de Mun, "The Fashion Show: Frocks Cut for Teen-Agers Displayed at Bonwit Teller," *New York Post*, 29 March 1944.
41. Ruth Carson, "Young and Gay," *Collier's Weekly*, 15 July 1944, 21.
42. Williams, *Fashion Is Our Business*, 50–51.
43. "Junior Fashions," *Vogue*, 1 October 1944, 161.
44. Bronwyn Cosgrave, *The Complete History of Costume & Fashion* (New York: Checkmark, 2000), 124.
45. "Junior Fashions," *Vogue*, 1 October 1944, 161.
46. Rathbone and Tarpley, *Fabrics and Dress*, 138.
47. Chambers, *Fashion Fundamentals*, 187.
48. Bonwit Teller, "New Designer."
49. "For the Teenager," *New York Times*, 30 August 1944.
50. "Resort News: Juniors in Knickerbockers," *Vogue*, 15 January 1946, 100.
51. Emily Wilkens Young Originals, "Young America."
52. Bonwit Teller, "New Designer."
53. Ibid.
54. Arnold, *American Look*, 118.
55. Emily Wilkens advertisement, "Emily Wilkens Young Originals: At the Finer Stores," *Harper's Bazaar*, January 1945, 24.
56. "Gabardine Suits, Young Black, Stars in Neiman-Marcus Teen Fashion Presentation," *Women's Wear Daily*, 7 February 1945.
57. "Resort Fashions," *Life*, 14 January 1947, 72.

CHAPTER 6

1. Emily Wilkens, *Here's Looking*, 40; *The Playbill*, "*Dear Ruth*," week beginning 30 September 1945, 35.

2. "Broadway in Review," *Theatre Arts*, vol. xxix, no. 6, (June 1945), 335.

3. Grayson, *Know Your Daughter?*, 28–29, 105.

4. Internet Broadway Database, "*Dear Ruth* Production Credits," http://www.ibdb. com/production.asp?id=1607; accessed 12 November 2007.

5. Krasna, *Dear Ruth*, 25–26.

6. "Gabardine Suits, Young Black, Stars in Neiman–Marcus Teen Fashion Presentation," *Women's Wear Daily*, 7 February 1945.

7. Wilkens, *Here's Looking*, 2.

8. Ibid., 3.

9. Williams, *Fashion Is Our Business*, 48.

10. Pope, "Designer's Career."

11. "A Modern and an Old-Fashioned Girl," *New York Times*, 29 March 1944.

12. Susan Porter Benson, *Counter Cultures: Saleswomen, Managers, and Customers in American Department Stores 1890–1940* (Urbana and Chicago: University of Illinois Press, 1986), 130.

13. Lambert, *World of Fashion* , 284.

14. Chambers, *Fashion Fundamentals*, 169; Virginia Pope, "Fashion Awards Bestowed Upon 3," *New York Times*, 14 February 1945; "Fashion Awards," *Life*, 26 February 1945, 33.

15. Chambers, *Keys*, 86.

16. Chambers, *Fashion Fundamentals*, 169; Pope, "Fashion Awards Bestowed Upon 3"; "Fashion Awards," *Life*, 26 February 1945, 33.

17. "Fashion Show of Award-Winning Designers Illustrates Oriental Tendencies Via L-85 Lines," *Women's Wear Daily*, 14 February 1945.

18. Wilkens, *Here's Looking*, 1.

19. "Fashion Awards," *Life*, 26 February 1945, 33.

20. Sandra Stansbery Buckland, "Promoting American Fashion 1940 Through 1945: From Understudy to Star" (PhD diss., Ohio State University, 1996), 19; Milbank, *New York Fashion*, 130–133.

21. Martin, *American Ingenuity*, 76; Richard Martin, "With Bustle," Dr. Sylvia S. Riskin Project in the Politics of Fashion, (New York: The Vera List Center for Art & Politics, New School University, 1999), 12–16; Milbank, *New York Fashion*, 146, 158.

22. "Fashion Awards," *Life*, 26 February 1945, 33; Martin, *American Ingenuity*, 10, 93.

23. "Summer Puts Junior Fashions in Romantic Mood," *Women's Wear Daily*, 7 February 1945.

24. "Fashion Awards," *Life*, 26 February 1945, 33.

25. This information was included on the catalogue card from the Costume Institute's acquisition of one of the eyelet-trimmed striped dresses from Wilkens's Spring/Summer 1945 collection.

26. *Harper's Bazaar, Junior Bazaar*, July 1945, 62.

27. "Kate Greenaway Styles," *Life*, 9 April 1945, 88; Saks Fifth Avenue advertisement, *New York Herald Tribune*, 20 September 1942.

28. Rebecca A. Perry, "'Girlies' and 'Grannies': The Influence of Kate Greenaway on Historical Styles of Girls' Dress in Late Nineteenth-Century Great Britain" (MA thesis, Bard Graduate Center, 2010), 1, 3, 63, 64.

29. "A Modern and an Old-Fashioned Girl," *New York Times*, 29 March 1944; Chambers also notes that Wilkens likes to show her interpretations of historical fashion side by side with her design, *Fashion Fundamentals*, 187; Martin, *American Ingenuity*, 93.

30. Williams, *Fashion Is Our Business*, 51. As someone who has taught History of Western Costume to aspiring designers, I completely agree with Wilkens that it is imperative for a fashion designer to have a good working knowledge of fashion history.

31. Martin, *American Ingenuity*, 93.

32. "The American Ballet Girl Look," *Vogue*, 1 February 1945, 150–151; *Vogue* advertisement, "*Vogue*: The Ballet Girl Look," *Women's Wear Daily*, 13 February 1945.

33. Martin, "With Bustle," 16.

34. "Draped Sleeves, Smock, Topper, Emily Wilkens Summer Designs," newspaper clipping, 7 February 1945, Fairchild Archive Emily Wilkens Designer Scrapbook.

35. Martin, "With Bustle," 15. C.I.41.2.1 is the dress's Costume Institute accession number.

36. "Draped Sleeves, Smock, Topper, Emily Wilkens Summer Designs," newspaper clipping, 7 February 1945, Fairchild Archive Emily Wilkens Designer Scrapbook.

37. Patricia R. Loughridge and Edward D.C. Campbell, Jr., *Women in Mourning* (Richmond, VA: Museum of the Confederacy, 1985), 12; Lou Taylor, *Mourning Dress: A Costume and Social History* (London: George Allen & Unwin, 1983), 178–179.

38. Martin, "With Bustle," 15.

39. Ibid.

40. "Fashion Awards," *Life*, 26 February 1945, 33.

41. Pope, "Designer's Career."

42. Virginia Pope, "Accent on Juniors," *New York Times*, 10 June 1951, SM18.

43. Burris-Meyer, *This Is Fashion*, 121.

44. The Walt Disney Family Museum, *The Walt Disney Family Museum: The Man, The Magic, The Memories* (New York: Disney Editions, 2009), 62.

45. Dorothy Shaver, Preface, in Edouard Halouze, *Costumes of South America* (New York: French & European Publications, 1941), n.p.

46. Virginia Pope, "New Styles in Old Found in Museums," *New York Times*, 25 October 1945.

47. Ibid.

48. "New Young Styles," *Life*, 18 March 1946, 87–88.

49. Ibid.

50. Everfast, Emily Wilkens Young Originals advertisement, *Vogue*, 1 January 1946, 31.

51. Emily Wilkens Young Originals advertisement, "Press Acclaims Emily Wilkens," *Women's Wear Daily*, 5 April 1944.

52. "Teen Dress Interest Stimulated in New York," *Women's Wear Daily*, 19 April 1944.

53. *Sheldon's Manufacturing*, 44th ed., 106, 107.

54. Virginia Pope, "Teen-age Fashions," *New York Times*, 1 October 1944.

55. Ibid.

56. Teen-timers, Inc., advertisement, "Two Loves for Doves," *Calling All Girls*, January–February 1945, 67.

57. *Kiplinger's*, "Teenagers as Customers," 33.

58. Teentimer Originals advertisement, "'Hot Stuff' for Teen Buyers," *Women's Wear Daily*, 12 April 1944.

59. *Sheldon's Manufacturing (Cutting Up) Trade*, 58th ed. (New York: J. S. Phelon, 1954), 162.

60. In my thinking about the way in which Wilkens's modern and historicizing designs were reassuring to the American public, I owe a debt to Karal Ann Marling's analysis of the architecture of Walt Disney's Disneyland. Karal Ann Marling, *Designing Disney's Theme Parks: The Architecture of Reassurance* (Paris and New York: Flammarion, 1997), 79–86.

61. Pope, "Designer's Career"; Chambers, *Keys*, 86; Emily Wilkens advertisement, "Emily Wilkens Gratefully Acknowledges the Neiman Marcus Award for 1945," *Women's Wear Daily*, 5 September 1945.

62. Wilkens, *Here's Looking*, 65.

63. "9 Women and Ship Cited by Magazine," *New York Times*, 28 December 1945; "Mademoiselle Merit Awards," *Mademoiselle*, January 1946, 132.

64. "Dewey Presents Fashion Awards," *New York Times*, 9 October 1946; Pope,

"Designer's Career"; "9 Women and Ship Cited by Magazine," *New York Times*, 28 December 1945; Stuart, *American Fashion Industry*, 64.

65. Two years later, in the presidential election, Thomas Dewey would be the candidate mistakenly credited in a Chicago newspaper headline with defeating Truman.

66. "Dewey Presents Fashion Awards," *New York Times*, 9 October 1946.

CHAPTER 7

1. Stuart, *American Fashion Industry*, 32.
2. Massoni, *Fashioning Teenagers*, 28; Palladino, *Teenagers*, 90.
3. Massoni, *Fashioning Teenagers*, 38–40, 50.
4. Ibid., 60, 123.
5. Fitz-Gibbon, *Macy's, Gimbels, and Me,* 90–91.
6. Massoni, *Fashioning Teenagers*, 143.
7. "Teen-Age Magazine: New 'Junior Bazaar' Is Published by Junior Misses Working on the Floor," *Life*, 29 October 1945, 77.
8. Ibid., 79.
9. "Advertising News and Notes," *New York Times*, 19 November 1945.
10. Massoni, *Fashioning Teenagers*, 89.
11. Ibid.
12. Chambers, *Fashion Fundamentals*, 8–9.
13. Stuart, *American Fashion Industry*, 36.
14. Chambers, *Fashion Fundamentals*, 17.
15. Schrum, *Some Wore Bobby Sox*, 14.
16. Anne Rittenhouse, *The Well-Dressed Woman* (New York: Harper, 1924), 153.
17. Rathbone and Tarpley, *Fabrics and Dress*, v.
18. Ibid., 69–89; 251–258.
19. Ibid.
20. National Retail Dry Goods Association, *The Buyer's Manual*, rev. ed. (New York: National Retail Dry Goods Association, 1949), 70–71.
21. Ryan, *Your Clothes and Personality*, 116.
22. Office of Price Administration, *Retail Ceiling Prices for Certain Apparel and House Furnishings*, Maximum Price Regulation No. 580 (Washington, D.C.: Government Printing Office, 1945), 27; see for example, *Women's Wear Daily*, 15 March 1944, 18–19.
23. *Kiplinger's*, "Teenagers as Customers," 32.
24. Benson, *Counter Cultures*, 149; Estelle Hamburger, *Fashion Business: It's All Yours* (San Francisco: Canfield, 1976), 40–43; *Kiplinger's*, "Teenagers as Customers," 32. In interselling, a dress salesperson might take her customer

around the store to buy the accessories needed to make a complete ensemble. This increased the dress salesperson's sales total, but took sales credit away from the other departments, and interfered with departmental accounting.

25. "Selling Teen Age Coats and Suits," *Women's Wear Daily*, 5 April 1944.

26. Ibid.

27. William H. Baldwin, *The Shopping Book* (New York: Macmillan, 1938), 28, 30, 33.

28. Donovan, *Saleslady*, 23, 26,48–49, 56.

29. Benson, *Counter Cultures*, 290; Victoria Buenger and Walter L. Buenger, *Texas Merchant: Marvin Leonard and Fort Worth* (College Station: Texas A & M University Press, 1998), 41.

30. Benson, *Counter Cultures*, 290.

31. Carlyle, "Take Time for Teens."

32. Hortense Odlum, *A Woman's Place: The Autobiography of Hortense Odlum* (New York: Charles Scribner's Sons, 1940), 6.

33. National Retail Dry Goods Association, *The Buyer's Manual*, 3–4.

34. Byers, *Help Wanted—Female*, 128–29.

35. Odlum, *A Woman's Place*, 76, 92–94, 97–99, 102–105.

36. Carlyle, "Take Time for Teens."

37. Ibid.; "Emily Wilkens Teen Designs Featured in Bonwit Teller Show," *Women's Wear Daily*, 13 April 1944.

38. "Teen Age Buyers Plan Association," *Women's Wear Daily*, 10 March 1944; "Two Boise Stores Open New Teen Dept.," *Women's Wear Daily*, 1 March 1944.

39. Benson, *Counter Cultures*, 16.

40. Carlyle, "Take Time for Teens."

41. "Bonwit's Launches 'Young Originals,' Tween Teen Shop," *Women's Wear Daily*, 29 March 1944.

42. Ibid.

43. Isabella Taves, *Successful Women and How They Attained Success* (New York: E.P. Dutton, 1943), 142, 152–156.

44. Sara Pennoyer, *Maggie in Fashion* (New York: Dodd, Mead, and Co., 1961), 209.

45. Carlyle, "Take Time for Teens."

46. Ibid.

47. *Women's Wear Daily*, "Emily Wilkens Teen Designs."

48. Tom Mahoney and Rita Hession, *Public Relations for Retailers* (New York: Macmillan, 1949), 1.

49. *Kiplinger's*, "Teenagers as Customers," 32.

50. National Retail Dry Goods Association, *The Buyer's Manual*, 76–77.

51. Chambers, *Fashion Fundamentals*, 187.

52. Wilkens, *Here's Looking*, 51.

53. Ibid., 52.

54. Eugenia Sheppard, "Emily Wilkens Opens Showing for Teen Agers," clipping dated 27 August 1946, Fairchild Archive, Emily Wilkens Designer Scrapbook.

55. "Neiman Marcus Show Honors Teen Fashions," *Women's Wear Daily*, 12 September 1945.

56. Gimbels advertisement, "Inviting you to see a television review of Gimbels Philadelphia Second Annual Assembly of Famous Fashions," *New York Times*, 10 March 1945.

57. Milliken Woolens advertisement, "Pert! Emily Wilkens's Bow-Tie Dress," *Seventeen*, February 1947, 6. *Life* magazine reported model Pat Geoghegan to be "one of the prettiest debutantes in New York, models for fashion photographers in her spare time." "Party Season: New York Society Revives Prewar Holiday Gaiety," *Life*, 6 January 1947, 75.

58. Milliken Woolens advertisement, "Arrived! Vera Maxwell's Poet-Suit!" *Life*, 14 January 1947, 58; Milliken Woolens advertisement, "Classic! Rose Barrack's Torso Dress!" *Life*, 10 February 1947, 108.

59. Milliken, "Pert!"; See, for example, Sally Milgrim advertisement, "Forthcoming Fashions as Revealed by Sally Milgrim," *Vogue*, 1 January 1923, 136; "Capes, Capes," *Vogue*, 15 July 1941, 19; Kohle Yohannan, *Valentina: American Couture and the Cult of Celebrity* (New York: Rizzoli, 2009), 228.

CHAPTER 8

1. Wilkens, *More Secrets*, 103; Wilkens, *Secrets*, 104.

2. Lindy Woodhead, *War Paint: Madame Helena Rubinstein and Miss Elizabeth Arden: Their Lives, Their Times, Their Rivalry* (Hoboken, NJ: John Wiley & Sons, 2003), 221.

3. Woodhead, *War Paint*, 221–222.

4. Wilkens, *More Secrets*, 78, 103; Wilkens, *Secrets*, 78, 104.

5. Wilkens, *More Secrets*, 103; Wilkens, *Secrets*, 104.

6. "June Moon's Glow in Evening Styles; Easing Restrictions to Bring More Romance in Design and Emphasis on Detail," *New York Times*, 4 October 1946.

7. Ibid.

8. "Emily Wilkens Picks Everfast Ginghams," advertisement, 1944, Fairchild Archive Emily Wilkens Designer Scrapbook; "High Waist," *Vogue*, June 1946, 145; Virginia Pope, "Youthful Charm," *New York Times*, 1 December 1946.

9. Arnold, *American Look*, 137.

10. Virginia Pope, "Dresses Marked by Sophistication; Emily Wilkens Display

Shows She Is Growing Up, From a Fashion Standpoint," *New York Times*, 7 February 1947.

11. "Evening Hemlines Necklines," *Vogue*, 15 August 1946, 156.

12. Richard Martin and Harold Koda, *Christian Dior* (New York: The Metropolitan Museum of Art, 1996), 10; Esmeralda de Réthy and Jean-Louis Perreau, *Christian Dior: The Early Years 1947–1957* (New York: Vendome, 2001), 7.

13. Ernestine Carter, *With Tongue in Chic* (London: Michael Joseph, 1974), 75.

14. "Blanket Fashions," *Life*, 17 February 1947, 71; Virginia Pope, "Blankets Turned into Modish Garb," *New York Times*, 4 February 1947.

15. Pope, "Dresses Marked by Sophistication."

16. Bonwit Teller advertisement, *New York Times*, 11 April 1947.

17. Pope, "Dresses Marked by Sophistication."

18. Lucks, "Genealogy of Lucks"; Bellafante, "Emily Wilkens."

19. Jane Wilkens Michael, e-mail to author, 10 April 2012.

20. "The West Indies: Again They Offer Americans a Paradise of Lush Beauty," *Life*, 30 December 1946, 34.

21. Peter Moruzzi, *Havana Before Castro: When Cuba Was a Tropical Playground* (Salt Lake City, Utah: Gibbs Smith, 2008), 52.

22. "The West Indies: Again They Offer Americans a Paradise of Lush Beauty," *Life*, 30 December 1946, 36.

23. Michael e-mail, 10 April 2012.

24. Hugh Wilkens Levey in Hugh Wilkens Levey and Jane Wilkens Michael, interview by author, 23 May 2012.

25. Michael, "Estée!"

26. Benson, *Counter Cultures*, 205.

27. Ibid., 178.

28. Virginia Pope, "Patterns of the *Times*: American Designer Series; Emily Wilkens Offers Costume for a Girl Going to College," *New York Times*, 7 August 1950.

29. Wilkens, *Here's Looking*, n.p.

30. Lambert, "Emily Wilkens Biography," 3.

31. Lucks, "Genealogy of Lucks"; Pope, "Patterns of the *Times*."

32. Levey in Levey and Michael interview, 23 May 2012.

33. Ibid.

34. Byers, *Help Wanted—Female*, 145.

35. Richards, *Ready-to-Wear Industry*, 32.

36. Ibid., 26.

37. Pope, "Patterns of the *Times*."

38. Donovan, *Saleslady*, 4, 31.

39. Singer Sewing Machine Company, "The Secret of Beautiful Clothes and a Beautiful Home," (n.p.: 1948), 4, 15.
40. Pope, "Patterns of the *Times*."
41. Lambert, "Emily Wilkens Biography," 2; Pope, "Patterns of the *Times*."
42. "The Honeymoon Journey," *Harper's Bazaar*, April 1951, 189.
43. Wilkens, "Emily Wilkens Scoffs."
44. Ibid.
45. Massoni, *Fashioning Teenagers*, 149.
46. Sandra Ley, *Fashion for Everyone* (New York: Charles Scribner's Sons, 1975), 104. Ley also mistakenly credits Wilkens with the costume designs for the film version of *Junior Miss*, rather than the stage version.
47. "In the Young Manner," *New York Times*, 5 November 1950; Stuart, *American Fashion Industry*, 63; Fairchild Archive, Emily Wilkens Designer Scrapbook, clipping dated 15 May 1951; Bonwit Teller advertisement, "Young Charmer by Young Designer . . . Emily Wilkens," *The New Yorker*, 25 February 1950, 16.
48. Emily Wilkens advertisement, "Lovely with a Fresh New Feeling," *Boston Sun Herald*, 11 February 1951.
49. 530 Seventh Avenue, "History," http://530seventh.com/history, accessed 12 May 2013.
50. *Sheldon's Manufacturing*, 44th ed., 101.
51. *Sheldon's Manufacturing*, 58th ed., 104.
52. "Lingerie Theatrics," *Life*, 18 December 1950, 42.
53. "Fashion: Petticoat Is a 'Must' This Season," *New York Times*, 17 July 1951.
54. "Slim Skirts and Full in Young Group," *Women's Wear Daily*, 25 October 1951.
55. Fogarty, *Wife Dressing*, "About the Author" dust jacket blurb; *Kiplinger's*, "Teenagers as Customers," 33.
56. Bess V. Oerke, *Dress* (Peoria, IL: Chas. A. Bennett, 1956), 55.
57. Laura Baxter and Alpha Latzke, *Today's Clothing* (Chicago: J. B. Lippincott, 1949), 62.
58. Oerke, *Dress*, 55.
59. "Will Head Fashion Show For U.N. Child Aid Fund," *New York Times*, 5 September 1950.
60. "Doll Auction on Tuesday Will Aid Fund of Service Helping Handicapped Children, *New York Times*, 1 December 1950.
61. Emily Wilkens advertisement, "Lovely."
62. "Cotton Maid Bows at a Fashion Show," *New York Times*, 1 February 1951; "Sheaths and 'Toppits,'" *Women's Wear Daily*, 15 November 1950.
63. John B. Stetson Co. advertisement, "The Stetsonian—Right for Big Moments," *Life*, 17 February 1947, 87.

64. Fairchild Archive, Emily Wilkens Designer Scrapbook, clipping dated 1951 (given the show it describes, most likely June 14).

65. Kirkland, "Sportswear for Everywhere," 39.

66. Fairchild Archive, Emily Wilkens Designer Scrapbook, clipping dated 27 March 1951.

67. Fairchild Archive, Emily Wilkens Designer Scrapbook, clippings dated 15 May 1951, 1951 (likely June 14).

68. David E. Lazaro, "Beautiful Clothes: Violet Angotti, Twentieth-Century Dress Designer," *Dress* (2011), 52, 53.

69. Gloria Groom, ed., *Impressionism, Fashion, and Modernity* (New Haven and London: The Art Institute of Chicago and Yale University Press, 2012), 46–47.

70. Paige Marshall, "Profile for Spring," *Dodge News* 17, no. 4 (Spring 1952), 9; "Sheaths and 'Toppits,'" *Women's Wear Daily*, 15 November 1950.

71. "Retailers Upheld on Buying Policy," *New York Times*, 23 April 1952.

72. Fairchild Archive, Emily Wilkens Designer Scrapbook, Bonwit Teller advertisements, 15 August 1953.

73. "Linings of Paisley Used in New Suits," *New York Times*, 10 September 1953.

74. Fairchild Archive, Emily Wilkens Designer Scrapbook, Bonwit Teller advertisements, 15 August 1953.

75. Pope, "Patterns of the *Times*."

76. Wilkens, *Here's Looking*, 46, 72; Wilkens, *A New You*, 168, 175–178, 194.

77. Harold Koda and Andrew Bolton, *Chanel* (New York and New Haven: The Metropolitan Museum of Art and Yale University Press, 2005), 135; Caroline Rennolds Milbank, *Couture: The Great Designers* (New York: Stewart, Tabori & Chang, 1985), 120; Jennifer Harris, ed., *Textiles: 5,000 Years* (New York: Harry N. Abrams, 1993), 106; Lucy Johnston, *Nineteenth-Century Fashion in Detail* (London: V&A Publishing, 2009), 102.

78. Wilkens, *A New You*, 168.

79. Fairchild Archive, Emily Wilkens Designer Scrapbook, Bonwit Teller advertisements, 15 August 1953; "Linings of Paisley Used in New Suits," *New York Times*, 10 September 1953.

80. "Linings of Paisley Used in New Suits," *New York Times*, 10 September 1953.

81. Jasco New York LLC, "About Us," http://www.jascofabrics.com/about-us/, accessed 4 February 2013.

82. National Archives, "Teaching with Documents: FDR's Fireside Chat on the Purposes and Foundations of the Recovery Program," http://www.archives.gov/education/lessons/fdr-fireside/, accessed 11 February 2013; Richards, *Ready-to-Wear Industry*, 27.

83. "Fashion Enjoyment on Modest 1954 Money," *Vogue*, 15 February 1954, 62.

84. Bonwit Teller advertisement, "Bonwit's Young Charmers in Navy Wool by Our Own Emily Wilkens," *New York Times*, 22 December 1953.

85. "Cotton Gamut," *New York Times*, 28 February 1954.

86. Lord & Taylor advertisement, "The Mantle," *New York Times*, 14 September 1955.

87. Helen Fraser, ed., *The Charming Woman* (New York: The Barbizon School of Modeling, 1952).

88. Emily Wilkens, "20th Day: Teenage Success," in Fraser, *Charming Woman*, no. 2, 61. *Here's Looking at . . . You!* had included the narrative device of Wilkens conducting a makeover on her younger sister Barbara as a way of introducing Wilkens's philosophy of beauty.

89. Pope, "Patterns of the *Times*."

CHAPTER 9

1. Wilkens, *More Secrets*, 7; Wilkens, *Secrets*, 7.

2. Fairchild Archive, Emily Wilkens Designer Scrapbook, Elizabeth Gage, "The Promise of a New You," no source, 9 November 1965.

3. Levey and Michael interview, 23 May 2012; Michael interview, 22 March 2012.

4. Bellafante, "Emily Wilkens"; Fashion Institute of Technology, Course Catalogue, 1967–1968, 25; Fashion Institute of Technology, *Portfolio* Yearbook, 1967, 16; Emily Wilkens is subsequently listed as a trustee until the 1977 edition of the Course Catalogue, 139. Emily Wilkens's obituary in *Women's Wear Daily* states that she began teaching at FIT as early as 1956, but I could not substantiate this in the Course Catalogues. "Emily Wilkens," *Women's Wear Daily*, 11 December 2000.

5. Fashion Institute of Technology, Course Catalogue, 1963–1965, 21; Fashion Institute of Technology, Course Catalogue, 1960–1961; Fashion Institute of Technology, Course Catalogue, 1961–1963.

6. Fashion Institute of Technology, Course Catalogue, 1965–1967, 22.

7. Fashion Institute of Technology, *Portfolio* yearbooks, 1961–1971; for an example of Pope and Stout's yearbook appearances, see *Portfolio* 1961, 28, 47.

8. Michael interview, 22 March 2012.

9. Fashion Institute of Technology, Course Catalogue, 1965–1967, 26; Fashion Institute of Technology, "Honorary Chairs," http://www.fitnyc.edu/aspx/Content.aspx?menu=Past:InstitutionalAdvancement:HowToSupportFIT:EndowedFunds&blind=true, accessed 23 July 2009.

10. Wilkens, *New You*, 1.

11. Michael interview, 9 April 2012.

12. Lester Gaba, *The Art of Window Display* (New York: The Studio Publications, 1952), 8,11–12; Lester Gaba, *On Soap Sculpture* (New York: Henry Holt, 1935).

13. Michael interview, 9 April 2012.

14. Wilkens, *New You*, 225–226.

15. Ibid., 226.

16. Ibid., 219–221.

17. Fashion Institute of Technology, Course Catalogue, 1969–1970, 31.

18. Fashion Institute of Technology, *Portfolio* Yearbooks, 1961–1971.

19. Fashion Institute of Technology, Course Catalogue, 1970–1971, 12, 31; Fashion Institute of Technology, Course Catalogue, 1971–1972; Fashion Institute of Technology, Course Catalogue, 2011–2013, http://www.fitnyc.edu/files/pdfs/UGCat_11-13.pdf, accessed 23 October 2013.

20. Wilkens, *More Secrets*, 7.

21. Display Ad 73, "From now on, when you buy your Times buy your New York Daily Column, too," *New York Times*, 1 April 1968; Emily Wilkens, "A New You" column, *The Deseret News*, 11 May 1971.

22. King Features, undated press release, "Emily Wilkens: A New You," Emily Wilkens press scrapbook 1976–1981, Collection of Hugh Wilkens Levey and Jane Wilkens Michael.

23. See for example, Emily Wilkens, "A New You" column, "Yoga Eases Pain in the Neck," *The Chicago Sun-Times*, 9 December 1981.

24. "Deaths," *New York Times*, 13 August 1970.

25. "Hugh Wilkens Levey Marries Wendy Flink," *New York Times*, 24 June 1973.

26. Marjorie Tingley, Account Executive, The Communications Group, letter dated 1 August 1975, Emily Wilkens Press Scrapbook 1976–1981.

27. Emily Wilkens Press Scrapbook 1976–1981.

28. Emily Wilkens, *Secrets*, 1.

29. Localmedia, Emily Wilkens tour schedule, Sunday, January 23, 1977–Wednesday, January 26, 1977, Emily Wilkens Press Scrapbook 1976–1981.

30. Michael interview, 22 March 2012; Emily Wilkens Press Scrapbook 1976–1981.

31. Emily Wilkens, *More Secrets*, 1.

32. "Emily Wilkens," *Women's Wear Daily*, 11 December 2000.

33. Bellafante, "Emily Wilkens."

34. Martin, *American Ingenuity*, 93, 95.

35. Ibid.; "Emily Wilkens," *Women's Wear Daily*, 11 December 2000; "Paid Notice: Deaths: Wilkens Levey, Emily," *New York Times*, 3 December 2000.

36. Wilkens, *Here's Looking*, 10.

BOOKS, DISSERTATIONS, JOURNALS, MAGAZINES, PAMPHLETS, THESES, WEB SITES

Ager, Stanley. *The Butler's Guide to Running the Home and Other Graces*. New York: Clarkson Potter, 2012.

Albrecht, Donald. *The High Style of Dorothy Draper*. New York: Museum of the City of New York and Pointed Leaf Press, 2006.

American Girl. "American Girl Clothing; Matching in Style—and Spirit." http://store.americangirl.com/agshop/static/clothing.jsp, accessed 5 February 5, 2013.

Arnett, Jeffrey. *Emerging Adulthood: The Winding Road from Late Teens through the Twenties*. Oxford: Oxford University Press, 2004.

Arnold, Rebecca. *The American Look: Fashion, Sportswear and the Image of Women in 1930s and 1940s New York*. London and New York: I. B. Tauris, 2009.

Baldwin, William H. *The Shopping Book*. New York: Macmillan, 1938.

Baxter, Laura, and Alpha Latzke. *Today's Clothing*. Chicago: J. B. Lippincott, 1949.

Benson, Sally. *Junior Miss*. New York: Random House, 1939.

Benson, Susan Porter. *Counter Cultures: Saleswomen, Managers, and Customers in American Department Stores 1890–1940*. Urbana and Chicago: University of Illinois Press, 1986.

Blum, Dilys E. *Shocking! The Art and Fashion of Elsa Schiaparelli*. New Haven and London: Philadelphia Museum of Art and Yale University Press, 2003.

Bolton, Andrew and Harold Koda. *Schiaparelli and Prada: Impossible Conversations*. New York: The Metropolitan Museum of Art, 2012.

Bro, Margueritte Harmon. *Let's Talk About You*. New York: Doubleday, Doran & Co.: 1945.

Bryant, Bernice. *Future Perfect: A Guide to Personality and Popularity for the Junior Miss*. Indianapolis and New York: Bobbs-Merrill, 1944.

Buckland, Sandra Stansbery. "Promoting American Fashion 1940 Through 1945: From Understudy to Star." PhD diss., Ohio State University, 1996.

Buenger, Victoria, and Walter L. Buenger. *Texas Merchant: Marvin Leonard and Fort Worth*. College Station: Texas A & M University Press, 1998.

Burris-Meyer, Elizabeth. *This Is Fashion*. New York and London: Harper, 1943.

Byers, Margaretta. *Help Wanted—Female*. New York: Julian Messner, 1941.

Bynner, John. "Rethinking the Youth Phase of the Life-Course: The Case for Emerging Adulthood?" *Journal of Youth Studies* 8, no. 4 (December 2005), 367–384.

Calling All Girls. The Hecht Company advertisement. "Dress up—Slim down in our 'Chubby Girl' charmer." January/February 1945, 18.

———. Teen-Timers advertisement. "Two Loves for Doves." January–February 1945, 67.

Carlyle, Cora. "Take Time for Teens." *Women's Reporter*, November 1944, no page.

Carson, Ruth. "Young and Gay." *Collier's Weekly*, 15 July 1944, 20–21.

Carter, Ernestine. *With Tongue in Chic*. London: Michael Joseph, 1974.

Chambers, Bernice Gertrude. *Fashion Fundamentals*. Englewood Cliffs, NJ: Prentice-Hall, 1947.

———. ed. *Keys to a Fashion Career*. New York: McGraw-Hill, 1946.

Chodorov, Jerome, and Joseph Fields. *Junior Miss*. New York: Dramatists Play Service, 1942.

Cook, Daniel Thomas. *The Commodification of Childhood*. Durham and London: Duke University Press, 2004.

Cosgrave, Bronwyn. *The Complete History of Costume & Fashion*. New York: Checkmark, 2000.

Daché, Lilly. *Talking Through My Hats*. New York: Coward-McCann, 1946.

Davis, Harriet Eager. "Work Summers for Teenagers." *Parents'*, June 1945, 30, 126–30.

De Réthy, Esmeralda, and Jean-Louis Perreau. *Christian Dior: The Early Years 1947–1957*. New York: Vendome, 2001.

"Designer Prescribes Cottons for Growing Up Figures." *Cotton News*, July & August 1944.

Donovan, Frances R. *The Saleslady*. Chicago: University of Chicago Press, 1929.

Duff Gordon, Lady [Lucy Christiana]. *Discretions and Indiscretions*. London: Jarrolds, 1932.

Dunwell, Steve. *The Run of the Mill: A Pictorial Narrative of the Expansion, Dominion, Decline and Enduring Impact of the New England Textile Industry*. Boston: David R. Godine, 1978.

Estes, Eleanor. *The Hundred Dresses*. New York: Harcourt, 1944.

Falk, Janet L. "Porfolio: Gruppo, Levey & Co." http://www.janetlfalk.com/gl.html, accessed 23 June 2009.

Fashion Institute of Technology. Course Catalogues. 1960–1977.

———. "Honorary Chairs." http://www.fitnyc.edu/aspx/Content.aspx-?menu=Past:InstitutionalAdvancement:HowToSupportFIT:Endowed-Funds&blind=true, accessed 23 July 2009.

———. *Portfolio* Yearbook. New York: Fashion Institute of Technology, 1961–1971.

Fitz Gibbon, Bernice. *Macy's, Gimbels, and Me: How to Earn $90,000 a Year in Retail Advertising*. New York: Simon and Schuster, 1967.

530 Seventh Avenue. "History." http://530seventh.com/history, accessed 12 May 2013.

Fogarty, Anne. *Wife Dressing*. New York: Julian Messner, 1959.

Fraser, Helen, ed. *The Charming Woman*. New York: The Barbizon School of Modeling, 1952.

Frederick, Mrs. Christine. *Selling Mrs. Consumer*. New York: The Business Bourse, 1929.

Gaba, Lester. *The Art of Window Display*. New York: The Studio Publications, 1952.

———. *On Soap Sculpture*. New York: Henry Holt, 1935.

Goldstein, Gabriel M., and Elizabeth Greenberg, eds. *A Perfect Fit: The Garment Industry and American Jewry, 1860–1960*. Lubbock: Texas Tech University Press and Yeshiva University Museum, 2012.

Grayson, Alice Barr. *Do You Know Your Daughter?* New York: Appleton-Century, 1944.

Groom, Gloria, ed. *Impressionism, Fashion, and Modernity*. New Haven and London: The Art Institute of Chicago and Yale University Press, 2012.

Halouze, Edouard. *Costumes of South America*. New York: French & European Publications, 1941.

Hamburger, Estelle. *Fashion Business: It's All Yours*. San Francisco: Canfield, 1976.

Hankins, Dorothy. "Adolescence: What Is It?" *Parents'*. April 1945, 30–31, 88, 90, 92, 94.

Harling, Robert. *Steel Magnolias*. Garden City, NY: The Fireside Theatre, 1987.

Harper's Bazaar. Bonwit Teller advertisement. "Brown Wool Young Charmers." August 1951, 5.

————. Emily Wilkens Young Originals advertisement. "Emily Wilkens Young Originals: At the finer stores." *Harper's Bazaar*, January 1945, 24.

————. "The Honeymoon Journey." April 1951, 189.

————. Ponemah Mills advertisement. "Portrait of a young girl in a postwar fabric." March 1945, 133.

Harper's Bazaar, Junior Bazaar. "Do You Know a Soldier?" March 1945, 126–27.

————. "The Jumpers." September 1945, 144–45.

————. Photograph. July 1945, 62–63.

————. "Step into the Sun." May 1945, 93–95.

Harris, Jennifer. ed. *Textiles: 5,000 Years.* New York: Harry N. Abrams, 1993.

Hawes, Elizabeth. *Fashion is Spinach.* New York: Random House, 1938.

Hollander, Anne. *Seeing Through Clothes.* Berkeley: University of California Press, 1993.

Howell, Geraldine. *Wartime Fashion: From Haute Couture to Homemade, 1939–1945.* London: Berg, 2012.

Internet Broadway Database. "*Dear Ruth* Production Credits." http://www.ibdb.com/production.asp?id=1607 , accessed 12 November 2007.

————. "*Junior Miss* Production Credits." http://www.ibdb.com/production.asp?ID=1136, accessed 12 November 2007.

Jasco New York LLC. "About Us." http://www.jascofabrics.com/about-us/, accessed 4 February 2013.

Johnston, Lucy. *Nineteenth-Century Fashion in Detail.* London: V&A Publishing, 2009.

Kiplinger's Personal Finance. "Teenagers as Customers." June 1947, 31–33.

Koda, Harold, and Andrew Bolton. *Chanel.* New York and New Haven: The Metropolitan Museum of Art and Yale University Press, 2005.

Krasna, Norman. *Dear Ruth.* New York: Dramatists Play Service, 1944.

Lambert, Eleanor. *World of Fashion.* New York & London: R. R. Bowker, 1976.

Lazaro, David E. "Beautiful Clothes: Violet Angotti, Twentieth-Century Dress Designer." *Dress* 37 (2011), 39–56.

Leipzig, Sheryl Farnan, Jean L. Parsons, and Jane Farrell Beck. "It is a Profession that is New Unlimited and Rich: Promotion of the American Designer in the 1930s." *Dress* 35 (2008–2009), 32–47.

Ley, Sandra. *Fashion for Everyone.* New York: Charles Scribner's Sons, 1975.

Life. "Blanket Fashions." 17 February 1947, 71–72.

————. "The 'Cheapest' Dressmaker." 20 May 1946, 58G–58J.

————. "Fashion Awards: Californian wins critics' prize." 26 February 1945, 32–33.

————. John B. Stetson Co. advertisement. "The Stetsonian—Right for Big Moments." 17 February 1947, 87.

———. "Junior Miss." 19 October 1942, 80–82.

———. "Kate Greenaway Styles." 9 April 1945, 87–88.

———. "Lingerie Theatrics." 18 December 1950, 41–45.

———. Milliken advertisement. "Arrived! Vera Maxwell's Poet-Suit!" 14 January 1947, 58.

———. Milliken advertisement. "Classic! Rose Barrack's Torso Dress!" 10 February 1947, 108.

———. "New Young Styles." 18 March 1946, 87–88.

———. "Party Dresses." 10 December 1945, 78–82.

———. "Party Season: New York Society Revives Prewar Holiday Gaiety." 6 January 1947, 69–75.

———. "Resort Fashions." 14 January 1947, 69–76.

———. "Schoolgirl Walks into Theater and Comes Out with Lead in Hit Show." 15 December 1941, 103–109.

———. "Teen-Age Magazine: New 'Junior Bazaar' Is Published by Junior Misses Working on the Floor." 29 October 1945, 77–80.

———. "The West Indies: Again They Offer Americans a Paradise of Lush Beauty." 30 December 1946, 34–42.

Little, Sara. "Young America's Favorite Dress Designer Lives Here." *House Beautiful*, August 1945, 60–61.

Loughridge, Patricia R., and Edward D.C. Campbell, Jr. *Women in Mourning*. Richmond, VA: Museum of the Confederacy, 1985.

Lucks, Michael. "Genealogy of Lucks, Kai and Related Families: Emily Ann Wilkens." http://www.mlucks.com/genealogy/lucks/descend.php?person-ID=I3310&tree=6, accessed 21 March 2012.

Mademoiselle. "*Mademoiselle* Merit Awards." January 1946, 132–133.

Mahoney, Tom and Rita Hession. *Public Relations for Retailers*. New York: Macmillan, 1949.

Marling, Karal Ann. *Designing Disney's Theme Parks: The Architecture of Reassurance*. Paris and New York: Flammarion, 1997.

Marshall, Paige. "Profile for Spring." *Dodge News* 17, no. 4 (Spring 1952): 9.

Martin, Richard. *All-American: A Sportswear Tradition*. New York: Fashion Institute of Technology, 1985.

———. *American Ingenuity: Sportswear 1930s–1970s*. New York: The Metropolitan Museum of Art, 1998.

———. "With Bustle." Dr. Sylvia S. Riskin Project in the Politics of Fashion. New York: The Vera List Center for Art & Politics, New School University, 1999.

Martin, Richard, and Harold Koda. *Christian Dior*. New York: The Metropolitan Museum of Art, 1996.

Massoni, Kelley. *Fashioning Teenagers: A Cultural History of Seventeen Magazine.* Walnut Creek, CA: Left Coast Press, 2010.

McCardell, Claire. *What Shall I Wear? The What, Where, When and How Much of Fashion.* New York: Simon and Schuster, 1956.

Michael, Jane Wilkens. "Estée!" *Town and Country*, [no date] 82, 84.

Milbank, Caroline Rennolds. *Couture: The Great Designers.* New York: Stewart, Tabori & Chang, 1985.

———. *New York Fashion: The Evolution of American Style.* New York: Harry N. Abrams, 1989.

Milgrim, Sally. "Forthcoming Fashions as Revealed by Sally Milgrim." Advertisement. *Vogue*, 1 January 1923, 136.

———. "Pert! Emily Wilkens's Bow-Tie Dress." *Seventeen*, February 1947, 6.

Mitford, Nancy. *Love in a Cold Climate.* New York: The Modern Library, 1994.

Moruzzi, Peter. *Havana Before Castro: When Cuba Was a Tropical Playground.* Salt Lake City, Utah: Gibbs Smith, 2008.

Mower, Jennifer M. and Elaine L. Pedersen. "'Pretty and Patriotic': Women's Consumption of Apparel During World War II." *Dress* 39, no. 1 (2013): 37–54.

National Archives. "Teaching with Documents: FDR's Fireside Chat on the Purposes and Foundations of the Recovery Program." http://www.archives.gov/education/lessons/fdr-fireside/, accessed 11 February 2013.

National Retail Dry Goods Association. *The Buyer's Manual*, rev. ed. New York: National Retail Dry Goods Association, 1949.

———. *Twenty-Five Years of Retailing.* New York: Mullens and Tutrone, 1936.

The New Yorker. Bonwit Teller advertisement. "Young Charmer by Young Designer . . . Emily Wilkens." 25 February 1950, 16.

———. "A Woman of Thirteen." 29 November 1941, 39.

Odlum, Hortense. *A Woman's Place: The Autobiography of Hortense Odlum.* New York: Charles Scribner's Sons, 1940.

Oerke, Bess V. *Dress.* Peoria, IL: Chas. A. Bennett, 1956.

Office of Price Administration. *Retail Ceiling Prices for Certain Apparel and House Furnishings.* Maximum Price Regulation No. 580. Washington, D.C.: Government Printing Office, 1945.

Palladino, Grace. *Teenagers: An American History.* New York: Basic Books, 1996.

Parents'. Botany Worsted Mills advertisement. "Botany." February 1945, 133.

———. "Problems: Teenage" column. March 1945, 35.

Pennoyer, Sara. *Maggie in Fashion.* New York: Dodd, Mead, and Co., 1961.

———. *Polly Tucker: Merchant.* New York: Dodd, Mead and Co., 1937.

Perkins, Jeanne. "Emily Post." *Life*, 6 May 1946, 59–66.

Perry, Rebecca A. "'Girlies' and 'Grannies': The Influence of Kate Greenaway on

Historical Styles of Girls' Dress in Late Nineteenth-Century Great Britain." MA thesis, Bard Graduate Center, 2010.

The Playbill. "*Dear Ruth.*" Week beginning 30 September 1945.

———. "*Junior Miss.*" Week beginning October 18, 1942.

Pratt Institute. *Prattonia* Yearbook. Brooklyn, NY: Pratt Institute, 1938.

Rathbone, Lucy, and Elizabeth Tarpley. *Fabrics and Dress.* Cambridge, MA: The Riverside Press, 1943.

Richards, Florence S. *The Ready-to-Wear Industry 1900–1950.* New York: Fairchild, 1951.

Rinehart, Mary Roberts. *Bab: A Sub-Deb.* New York: George H. Doran, 1917.

Rittenhouse, Anne. *The Well-Dressed Woman.* New York: Harper, 1924.

Roberts, J. M. *The Penguin History of Europe.* London: Penguin, 1996.

Rudofsky, Bernard. *Are Clothes Modern?* Chicago: Paul Theobald, 1947.

Ryan, Mildred Graves. *Your Clothes and Personality*, 3rd ed. New York: Appleton-Century-Crofts, 1949.

Scheiner, Georganne. *Signifying Female Adolescence: Film Representations and Fans, 1920–1950.* Westport, CT, and London: Praeger, 2000.

Schrum, Kelly. *Some Wore Bobby Sox: The Emergence of Teenage Girls' Culture, 1920–1945.* New York: Palgrave-Macmillan, 2004.

Seventeen. "Precision Miniatures" and "Cinema Charm Manufacturers" advertisements. February 1947, 236.

Shaver, Dorothy. Preface. In Edouard Halouze. *Costumes of South America.* New York: French & European Publications, 1941.

Sheldon's Manufacturing (Cutting Up) Trade, 44th ed. New York: J. S. Phelon, 1940.

———. 58th ed. New York: J. S. Phelon, 1954.

Singer Sewing Machine Company. "The Secret of Beautiful Clothes and a Beautiful Home." n.p. 1948.

Stuart, Jessie. *The American Fashion Industry.* Boston: Simmons College, 1951.

Taves, Isabella. *Successful Women and How They Attained Success.* New York: E. P. Dutton, 1943.

Taylor, Lou. *Mourning Dress: A Costume and Social History.* London: George Allen & Unwin, 1983.

Theatre Arts. "Broadway in Review." vol. xxvi, no. 6 (June 1942): 397.

———. "Broadway in Review." vol. xxvi, no.1 (January 1942): 9–14.

———. "Broadway in Review." vol. xxix, no. 6. (June 1945): 334–35.

Tootsie Roll Industries. "Junior Mints Original." http://www.tootsie.com/products.php?pid=153; accessed 17 June 2011.

Tortora, Phyllis G., and Keith Eubank. *Survey of Historic Costume*, 5th ed. New York: Fairchild, 2010.

Tortora, Phyllis G., and Robert S. Merkel. Fairchild's Dictionary of Textiles, 7th ed. (New York: Fairchild, 2000)

Vienne, Veronique. "The Why of It All." *Metropolis Magazine*, November 2000. http://www.metropolismag.com/html/content_1100/tur.htm accessed 15 November 2007.

Vogue. "The American Ballet Girl Look." 1 February 1945, 150–154.

———. Bonwit Teller advertisement. "New Designer for the Teens . . . Emily Wilkens." 1 May 1944, 137. This same advertisement also ran in the *New York Times*, 16 April 1944.

———. "Capes, Capes." 15 July 1941, 19.

———. "Evening Hemlines Necklines." 15 August 1946, 156.

———. Everfast. Emily Wilkens Young Originals advertisement. 1 January 1946, 31.

———. "Fashion Enjoyment on Modest 1954 Money." 15 February 1954, 56–64.

———. "High Waist." June 1946, 144–145.

———. "Junior Fashions." 15 May 1944, 100–103.

———. "Junior Fashions." 1 June 1944, 144–145.

———. "Junior Fashions." 1 October 1944, 160–164.

———. "Resort news: Juniors in Knickerbockers." 15 January 1946, 100.

The Walt Disney Family Museum. *The Walt Disney Family Museum: The Man, The Magic, The Memories*. New York: Disney Editions, 2009.

Warburton, Gertrude and Jane Maxwell. *Fashion for a Living*. New York and London: McGraw-Hill, 1939.

Webber-Hanchett, Tiffany. "Dorothy Shaver: Promoter of 'The American Look.'" *Dress* 30 (2003): 80–90.

Wilkens, Emily. *Here's Looking at . . . You!* ed. Dorothy Roe Lewis. New York: G. P. Putnam's Sons, 1948.

———. *More Secrets from the Super Spas*. New York: Dembner, 1983.

———. *A New You: The Art of Good Grooming*. New York: G. P. Putnam's Sons, 1965.

———. "Reorganize Your Wardrobe in 10 Steps." *McCall's*, March 1948, 150–151.

———. *Secrets from the Super Spas*. New York: Grossett & Dunlap, 1976.

———. "Ten Little Yogas." Pamphlet. New York: King Features Syndicate.

Williams, Beryl. *Fashion Is Our Business*. Philadelphia: J. B. Lippincott, 1945.

Woodhead, Lindy. *War Paint: Madame Helena Rubinstein and Miss Elizabeth Arden: Their Lives, Their Times, Their Rivalry*. Hoboken, NJ: John Wiley & Sons, 2003.

Yeshiva University Museum. *A Perfect Fit: The Garment Industry and American Jewry 1860–1960*. New York: Yeshiva University Museum, 2005.

Yohannan, Kohle. *Valentina: American Couture and the Cult of Celebrity*. New York: Rizzoli, 2009.

Yohannan, Kohle, and Nancy Nolf. *Claire McCardell: Redefining Modernism*. New York: Harry N. Abrams, 1998.

ARCHIVAL SOURCES, OBJECTS, AND OTHER MEDIA

Arden, Elizabeth. Bed-Top Vanity. (Gift to Emily Wilkens.) Collection of Jane Wilkens Michael and Hugh Wilkens Levey.

Fairchild Archives. Emily Wilkens Designer Scrapbook.

Junior Miss. 1945 motion picture. Beverly Hills, CA: Twentieth Century Fox Home Entertainment, 2012. DVD.

Lambert, Eleanor. "Emily Wilkens Biography" press release. The Metropolitan Museum of Art, Costume Institute Library, vertical files. ocl 201490998.

Wilkens, Emily. Emily Wilkens Press Scrapbooks 1976–1981. Collection of Jane Wilkens Michael and Hugh Wilkens Levey.

Wilkens, Emily, with Lester Gaba. *A New You*. Home Makeover/Beauty Kit Prototype. Collection of Jane Wilkens Michael and Hugh Wilkens Levey.

INTERVIEWS AND CORRESPONDENCE

Levey, Hugh Wilkens, and Jane Wilkens Michael, interview by author, 23 May 2012.

Michael, Jane Wilkens. E-mail to author, 10 April 2012.

———. E-mail to author, 8 April 2013.

———. Interview by author, 22 March 2012.

———. Interview by author, 9 April 2012.

Office of the Registrar, Pratt Institute, e-mail to author, dated 19 April 2013.